What people are saying about …

gotta have it!

"Gregg Jantz's coined word, *excessity*, pushes readers to examine what drives them to real-but-extreme wants and yearnings. As he points out, if we don't have our true needs met, the drug of excessities deadens our pain in our failed attempts to find happiness."

Cecil Murphy, speaker and coauthor of the *New York Times* best seller *90 Minutes in Heaven*

"This book will help just about anyone identify three core life issues—what you want, what you really need, and what God provides. When these three compass points are aligned, it's easier to live a life full of contentment, peace, and satisfaction."

Dr. Tim Clinton, president of the American Association of Christian Counselors

"Are you burdened, discouraged, and worn down? Are you tired of the never-ending crusade to aspire, struggle to achieve, and strain to attain? Dr. Gregg Jantz masterfully exposes the subtle lure of life's 'excessities' and their corrosive impact on mind, body and spirit, and provides a simple yet effectual guide to freedom, health, and peace!

Timothy R. Jennings, MD, Christian psychiatrist, speaker, radio personality, and author of *Could It Be This Simple?*

"This is a very helpful book that exposes our excessities (when excesses become necessities) in areas such as food, alcohol, caffeine, electronics, shopping, exercise, hobbies, gambling, sex, relationships, and money. It also provides biblically-based solutions centered in God and what He provides: patience, endurance, contentment, wisdom, hope, help, and answers."

Rev. Dr. Siang-Yang Tan, professor of psychology
at Fuller Theological Seminary and senior pastor
of First Evangelical Church in Glendale, CA

gotta have it!

gotta have it!

freedom *from* wanting *everything*
RIGHT HERE, RIGHT NOW

Gregory L. Jantz, PhD

WITH ANN MCMURRAY

transforming lives together

GOTTA HAVE IT!
Published by David C. Cook
4050 Lee Vance View
Colorado Springs, CO 80918 U.S.A.

David C. Cook Distribution Canada
55 Woodslee Avenue, Paris, Ontario, Canada N3L 3E5

David C. Cook U.K., Kingsway Communications
Eastbourne, East Sussex BN23 6NT, England

David C. Cook and the graphic circle C logo
are registered trademarks of Cook Communications Ministries.

The Web site addresses recommended throughout this book are offered as a
resource to you. These Web sites are not intended in any way to be or imply an
endorsement on the part of David C. Cook, nor do we vouch for their content.

The names mentioned throughout this book have been changed for privacy purposes.

All Scripture quotations, unless otherwise noted, are taken from the *Holy
Bible, New International Version*®. *NIV*®. Copyright © 1973, 1978, 1984
by International Bible Society. Used by permission of Zondervan. All
rights reserved. Scripture quotations marked msg are taken from *THE
MESSAGE*. Copyright © by Eugene H. Peterson 1993, 1994, 1995, 1996,
2000, 2001, 2002. Used by permission of NavPress Publishing Group.

LCCN 2010925762
ISBN 978-1-4347-6624-3
eISBN 978-1-4347-0242-5

© 2010 Gregory L. Jantz, PhD

The Team: Gudmund Lee, Susan Tjaden, Amy Kiechlin,
Sarah Schultz, Caitlyn York, Karen Athen
Cover design: Lucas Art and Design, John Lucas
Cover photo: Veer Images, royalty-free

Printed in the United States of America
First Edition 2010

1 2 3 4 5 6 7 8 9 10

042910

This book is dedicated to The Center Team—an amazing group of caring professionals who faithfully partner for the benefit of those we serve. Together we are able to lead people into positive life changes and freedom from strongholds.

Contents

Acknowledgments 11

Introduction 13

SECTION 1: The Power of Wants **19**

1. A Toddler's Tale 21

2. Examine Your Excess 35

SECTION 2: Our True Needs **65**

3. Our Need for Comfort 67

4. Our Need for Reassurance 87

5. Our Need for Security 107

6. Our Need for Validation 123

7. Our Need for Control 137

SECTION 3: What God Provides **157**

8. God Provides Patience 159

9. God Provides Endurance 177

10. God Provides Contentment 189

11. God Provides Wisdom 199

12. God Provides Hope 215

13. God Provides Help 231

14. God Provides Answers 249

Afterword 259

Notes 263

Books by Gregory L. Jantz, PhD 265

Acknowledgments

Writing this book has been a joy on so many levels, especially working with special individuals with such helpful talents and encouraging enthusiasm.

I was surprised and delighted to have Susan Tjaden as my editor for this project. Susan, after knowing each other for twelve years, who could have imagined you would edit this book!

Don Pape at David C. Cook is someone I have admired for many years. Don, thank you for putting together the vision and team at Cook to bring this book to print.

Ann McMurray has worked together with me so faithfully over the years. Ann, thank you for making sure my heart is reflected on every page.

Thank you to our heavenly Father, who is our Comforter and the Provider of all our needs.

Introduction

In 1986, the self-proclaimed president of the Philippines, Ferdinand Marcos, was deposed in a coup because he was more dictator than president. A public sick and tired of Marcos's dictatorial attitudes and excesses hounded him and his wife, Imelda, off the island republic. Ferdinand and Imelda were unceremoniously flown from the capital city of Manila aboard a U.S. government helicopter, barely ahead of a horde of angry citizens.

Amid the remarkable events of that day, people took notice of the black espadrilles Imelda Marcos wore as she boarded the helicopter. Why would anyone focus on footwear when an entire country was enmeshed in such momentous events? It turns out the concern wasn't over a single pair of shoes, but rather on the fact that Imelda Marcos had over one thousand pairs of shoes.

When the dictator's palace gates were breached and Imelda Marcos's private closets thrown open to the world, news of her shoes hit the media. There were rows upon rows of shoes, in an astonishing display of color and style. She also had fur coats and gowns and handbags, but the shoes were what really captured the public's attention. Why would anybody have so many? Some would say she had a shoe obsession. I think we can all agree that Imelda regularly, extravagantly, excessively binged on shoes.

Any reasonable, rational person could conclude that having over a thousand pairs of shoes is unnecessary. However, Imelda Marcos was hardly reasonable or rational about her shoes. To Imelda, her shoes were a *necessity*. She justified her behavior by saying she was merely helping the Philippine shoe industry. She refused to accept any concept of excess where her shoes were concerned. One pair of shoes, possibly even a couple of pairs, is a necessity. A thousand pairs of shoes, I hope you'll come to recognize, is an *excessity*.

LOOKING AT OUR OWN DESIRES, WANTS, AND NEEDS

It's quite easy to shake our heads and joke about Imelda Marcos's shoes. And the world did that for a brief moment of time in the late eighties after going through the closets of her life. Even today, we can look at her behavior from a safe distance of time and place and comment on the woman who was out of control where her shoes were concerned.

When we start looking at our own behavior, however, that zone of safety shrinks. Yet the point of this book is to learn to distinguish between true *needs* and *wants*. We'll talk about life's *excessities*— a made-up word for a very real situation for many people, when excesses become necessities. This book is about the compulsion to overindulge in any number of everyday behaviors, including the bizarre, comical, and the not so funny. Excessity is the impulse that throws caution to the wind and demands immediate satisfaction. It is the blindness that occurs when comfort becomes more important than consequences.

Excessity is about feeding our wants and desires, while at the same time starving our true needs. The more we starve what we really need, the greater our hunger grows, causing us to stuff ourselves with more and more of our wants. After stuffing ourselves full of our wants, we find that we're still starving, empty, and desperate—and the mad cycle repeats.

Excessities show up in a variety of styles, just like Imelda's shoes. But when we look at this behavior here, it won't be from the safety of a front-page story or a past time or a faraway place; it will be close up, right now, in our own lives and the lives of those we love.

GETTING THE MOST OUT OF THIS BOOK

Gotta Have It! is divided into three sections. Section 1 helps us identify those things that we've declared are an absolute personal necessity in life. It will also help identify if a necessity is—or has the potential to become—an overpowering excessity.

After identifying the truth behind our desires and wants, we're going to take a look at our true needs in section 2. I will warn you up front that we are not the best judges of what our true needs are. Therefore, we're also going to look at what God has to say about true needs and about wants and desires. When it comes to a plumb line for measuring whether or not something is a true need, we're going to use God's Word rather than relying on our own understanding or emotions. Take a deep breath now because this won't be easy.

Section 3 is a reminder of the amazing provision of God in our lives. It will also help you to see the wisdom in letting go of some things so that you're prepared to grab hold of others much more valuable.

Yes, this book is about wants and needs, but it's also about much more. The only way to get what we truly need is to surrender our needs to God. It's kind of like the Seed Principle, which Jesus explains in John 12:24–25: "I tell you the truth, unless a kernel of wheat falls to the ground and dies, it remains only a single seed. But if it dies, it produces many seeds. The man who loves his life will lose it, while the man who hates his life in this world will keep it for eternal life." The Seed Principle says *give up to get.*

We're so busy scrambling after the single seeds in our lives that we fail to experience the bountiful harvest God intends, starving ourselves instead. True fulfillment comes through seeking God's kingdom and His righteousness. When we follow this path, God, who knows our needs, supplies them and give us much more. Filled up with God's "much more," our drive to turn excesses into necessities, or *excessities*, diminishes.

Each of the chapters in this book includes a "Planting Seeds" section. It will consist of actions for you to take and scriptural insights for you to study as you seek to put the Seed Principle into practice, learning what to give up so you can have more. It can also function as a study guide for each chapter and will include some directed questions to help you apply what you've read. You are welcome to do this individually or together with a group of friends as a way to build fellowship, transparency, and accountability.

You'll notice I've used the word *you,* but I've also used the word *we* quite a bit so far. I'm going to continue to do so because I'm not writing this from a lofty pedestal perch. As a human being who also confuses the line between wants and needs, I'm right there with you. However, I am getting better at discerning the difference between a necessity and an excessity. True, I have the benefit of a doctorate in counseling psychology, but I've also had the privilege of walking this path with many people over the past twenty-five years, and I've learned a thing or two along the way. Those things are what I'm going to share with you in *Gotta Have It!*

Dr. Gregg Jantz

Please note, I fully anticipate that some of you will be able to go through the exercises in this book on your own or with the help of a good friend or family member. I understand, however, that many of you will not. The issues being brought up to the surface for some will require professional counseling and assistance. I urge you to contact the American Association of Christian Counselors and look for professional Christian help in your area. By all means, use this book as a tool to navigate through these issues with your counselor or therapist.

Section 1

The Power of Wants

The first section of this book will help you identify the difference between what you need and what you want. There is a universal nature to *needs*. We all need air to breathe, food to eat, some sort of shelter. Needs fold us into the human community because they apply to just about everyone. Wants, however, are much more individualized. You can learn a great deal about a person just by hearing him or her say, "I want that," and paying attention to what "that" is.

In this section, you'll become much more aware of where, when, how often, and about what you say, "I want that." This understanding is important because wants are powerful. You'll see that saying, "I want that," is really a confession of desire. Because desire is incredibly strong, it has the power to charge excessities. When a want becomes supercharged it can start to feel like a need. Unfortunately, if you determine that a destructive behavior corresponds to a need, you will resist giving it up, and the damage will continue. However, if you can identify it as a want, then you can address the true need behind the want and modify your behavior.

1

A Toddler's Tale

These are rebellious people, deceitful
children, children unwilling to listen to
the LORD's instruction. (Isa. 30:9)

Who hasn't viewed an irate toddler in a store, yelling at the top of his tiny lungs, demanding the object of his heart's desire? In the mind of that boy, he *needs* the candy, the toy, the bag, the box, or whatever. In his mind, what he wants is what he needs.

Recently, I found myself in the grocery store at the end of a long day, needing to pick up milk on my way home from work. I was tired, distracted, and just wanted to be home. It turns out I wasn't the only unhappy person in that store. A couple of aisles over, a little girl began keening loudly. I admit, grocery stores are incubators of human nature that I find irresistible, so—milk temporarily forgotten—I walked over to observe.

Usually I'm most interested in how the adult in the situation deals with the child. Believe me, over the years I've seen a variety of styles—some that have made me smile and some that have made me cringe. This time, however, I was focused on the child. This two-year-old was gesturing desperately, fingers extended, at some object just out of reach. The important thing to me wasn't what she was looking at, but rather how she was seeing it. In her mind, the object wasn't a mere *want*—it had become a *need*. When her mother denied it to her, she became absolutely bereft, carrying on in a way only a despondent, denied toddler can.

As I made my way to the dairy section, through the checkout line, and back into my car, I kept thinking about how this kind of behavior is typical of small children. But I had to ask myself—do we ever really get over that?

Fast-forward into adulthood, and you'll find the same thing: *wants* masquerading as *needs*. When we were two, we cried out to a parent to fill our heartfelt desires; as adults we endeavor to fill them ourselves. Once a desire has been categorized as a need, we're pretty resourceful at finding a way to fill it—even when our methods are addictive, damaging, or hurtful. In our current credit-card-toting, get-it-now-but-pay-for-it-later society, we're about as happy with the words *no* and *not now* as that bawling two-year-old.

Add to that our concept of "rights." Once we've identified a desire as a need, we tend to demand the right to fill that need. Deep down, we seem to acknowledge that a desire doesn't quite meet the level of a basic need. Desires can be selfish, but a need is always a moral necessity. Once our desire gets translated into a need, it becomes a necessity in our lives; we're pretty militant about getting that newly defined need met.

This leads me to a question: Are you ready to take a deep, hard look at your own self-identified needs? I've found generally people haven't really done any sort of intentional, directed work in this area.

Mainly, they have a vaguely articulated sense of what they consider needs in their lives. Sometimes the only true way to determine how you really look at a particular aspect of your life—as a desire or as a need—is through your behaviors and your willingness or unwillingness to change. We're willing to change, postpone, modify, or even relinquish a desire; we tend to take an over-my-dead-body approach to anything we think is a need.

Lest you think this book is only going to be about what *you* think or *I* think, I want to establish the overriding theme we'll be using, which doesn't come from you or me. The theme of this book comes from Jesus, speaking to a crowd of people very much like us, with desires and needs and a difficult time differentiating between the two. They were just as apt to run after desires masquerading as needs. In Matthew 6:31–33, Jesus said, "So do not worry, saying, 'What shall we eat?' or 'What shall we drink?' or 'What shall we wear?' For the pagans run after all these things, and your heavenly Father knows that you need them. But seek first his kingdom and his righteousness, and all these things will be given to you as well." Even if we don't have a good handle on what our needs are, God does. And not only is He God; He's also our Father. And as a father, He's generous. He knows our needs, and He has a plan to supply them—and much more as well.

BACKGROUND NOISE

Have you ever experienced the sheer relief that silence brings? There are days, with two rambunctious boys in my house, when the noise reaches an incredible decibel. Now don't get me wrong; I love to be right there in the mix with them. But there's something about the calm and serenity silence brings. There are times silence is just what my jangled senses need to be still and hear God.

In some ways, all of the excessities of life come with their own noise. They fill up our lives but leave no room for silence and contemplation, for rest and relief. God, when He fills us up, does so through a whisper, through the breath of the Spirit. A little of God goes a lot further than a great deal of anything else. The psalmist put it this way in Psalm 84:10: "Better is one day in your courts than a thousand elsewhere." When we feed on God, we diminish our compulsion to binge on anything else. Just as a toddler must trust a parent to know how to supply true needs, we, as children of God, must look to our heavenly Father to do the same. Our challenge is to approach God, our Father, with the faith and trust of a child.

THE BOTTOM LINE FROM JOB

The Old Testament book of Job is a story about a man who faced this question of what is a desire and what is a need. This man, Job, is literally stripped of all of the things that made up his life. It is not an easy book to read or understand, but it's very instructive in determining desires versus needs.

At the beginning of the book God and Satan have a discussion about Job, and God agrees to allow Satan to test Job's commitment to God. In the first test, God allows Satan to take away all of Job's possessions, including his children, but doesn't allow him to harm Job physically. In the course of a single day, all of Job's livestock, sheep, camels, servants, and children are killed or taken away from him. At the end of this single day, Job still praises God.

Not to be deterred, Satan comes again and this time asks to remove Job's health from him. God agrees but says Satan may not take his life. Satan promptly strikes Job with painful boils from head to foot.

God establishes the bottom line with Satan where Job is concerned. Throughout the book of Job, no matter what else happens to him, Job has his physical needs met enough for him to continue to live. Job's desires for understanding, vindication, relief, and restoration have to wait. With nearly everything taken away from him, it becomes clearer to see what constitutes a true need. In our own lives, we need that kind of clarity.

UNRAVELING NEEDS AND WANTS

It can be very difficult to determine what you consider a desire and a need in your life. When asked, you may give what you think should be the right answer instead of the truth. You may admit, reluctantly, that you don't really need your morning coffee. However, when faced with the choice of being late to work because the line at the Starbucks is eight cars deep or going without your morning beverage ... well ... "It's just work." You may concede that your late-night snack of cookies and ice cream is not really a need, but you'll leave your house at 9:47 at night with a coat over your pajamas to drive to the store in order to replenish your Ben & Jerry's.

Desires are things you want; you can do without them, but you still want them. Life goes on in their absence, but having them would certainly enhance it. Needs, however, have a greater sense of urgency. A desire deferred is inconvenient, even uncomfortable, but a need denied is deprivation. So, how can we trust that what we define as a need is really a need? And how can we be honest about what category our perceived needs actually fall into?

It's difficult for us to put ourselves in Job's position because of the extreme devastation of what Job initially experienced. So let's go for something a little bit easier. I'd like you to take a moment and think about life on a desert island. I'm not really thinking of the Swiss Family Robinson type of island. If you've seen the movie *Cast Away* with Tom Hanks, this is the picture I'm working toward. I want you to picture yourself stranded on a desert island, in the middle of nowhere, with very few resources. You need to survive—yes, survival is a bona fide need. So, what do you need to survive? (Because you're on the planet, assume you've got something to breathe so you can move past that most primal need of life: oxygen.) Write down your top three needs:

What I would *need* in order to survive:

1.

2.

3.

If I were to answer this question myself, I'd say water, food, and shelter are my primary needs. Actually, these are pretty much what Jesus mentioned in the Matthew 6 passage. He put it as *what to eat, what to drink,* and *what to wear.* (Clothing is really a form of shelter, so I'm going to accept the similarity.) Those are pretty basic. In fact, outside of this prosperous nation of ours, a good deal of the human population spends a large portion of its time and energy searching after these basic needs. Go too long without water and you die of thirst. Go too long without food and you die of hunger. Go too long without shelter and you die of exposure. Needs can be determined by how essential they are to sustaining life.

Ahhhh, there's the dilemma, isn't it? When we consider what is essential to life, we aren't always talking about physical life, are we? We have an emotional, relational, and spiritual life to go with this physical one. So, go back and relabel your needs list as "My Physical Needs."

Now, I want you to come up with at least three needs under each of the other categories.

My Emotional Needs:

    1.

    2.

    3.

My Relational Needs:

    1.

    2.

    3.

My Spiritual Needs:

    1.

    2.

    3.

Under emotional needs, you might have such things as optimism, hope, joy. Relational needs might include things like acceptance, affirmation, forgiveness. And for spiritual needs, perhaps you listed things like faith, trust, praise. I share these with you not to say that these are definitive answers, but to give you an idea of the types of things you could choose. Again, I find that many people have never done this type of inventory, let alone put intentional thought into dealing with these types of questions.

Going back to our desert-island exercise, we've already established what our physical needs are, but as Jesus said in Luke 4:4, referencing Deuteronomy 8:3, "Man does not live on bread alone." So, let's say you've got your physical needs taken care of. You've got food to eat, water to drink, and shelter from the elements. What other three things would you personally want (or desire) to survive on that island?

What I would *want* in order to survive:

    1.

    2.

    3.

After thinking about it myself, here's what I'd want: a Bible, a purpose, and a chance of escape. Even though we've categorized these as wants (or desires), they're still pretty important. I doubt any of you would seriously put lattes and ice cream on this list. When reduced to choices of these kinds, those behaviors are pretty easy to label.

Short of being stranded on a desert island or experiencing a Job-type catastrophe, it can be difficult to stop long enough to make sense of our busy lives. That's what this book is designed to help you do. In the next chapter, we're going to start by looking at the most common ways I've seen over my twenty-five years in counseling that people try to fill themselves up. These ways all have a similar "if some is good, more is better" deception, leading to compulsive, impulsive behavior.

Next, we're going to begin to identify our real needs because every person who engages in excessive behavior has a true need at the core of that behavior. By discovering what those core needs are, we can detach the power of the need from the excess of the behavior and begin meeting the need in a positive, healing way. Finally, we'll look at the gifts God gives us to meet our true needs. We'll bring the words of Jesus from Matthew 6 full circle and learn how to live with our needs fulfilled as we seek His kingdom and His righteousness.

Planting Seeds

In this chapter, we looked at the story of Job. Let's use this to go deeper into Scripture.

At the end of the first chapter of Job, he finds out that his physical possessions and his children have been taken away from him. He responds by saying in Job 1:21, "Naked I came from my mother's womb, and naked I will depart. The LORD gave and the LORD has taken away; may the name of the LORD be praised."

1. If you were reduced down to the bare essentials like Job was, what would you still have left from the Lord?

2. How do these bare essentials help you determine the difference between a desire and a need? (For example, you might desire to cover your nakedness with something soft, but your need is only for a covering.)

3. When God's provisions were taken away, Job was able to see them more clearly. In your own life, have you experienced a time when you were stripped to the bare essentials? What did you lose, and what did you have left? In the midst of your loss, what was the one thing you clung to the most?

4. In Job 1:22, the chapter ends with this statement: "In all this, Job did not sin by charging God with

wrongdoing." What has your response been when a desire of yours has not been met? Have you praised God, like Job? Have you blamed God? Have you charged God with "wrongdoing" in your life?

5. Is your reaction to an unfulfilled desire the same as to an unmet need? Does the impact to your life *feel* the same to you? Is your response to God the same?

6. The second test Job deals with is the loss of physical health. How would you categorize physical health for yourself? Do you desire to be physically healthy, or do you consider physical health a necessity?

7. When Job was faced with severe physical complications, he accepted his condition and refused to, as his wife suggested, "curse God and die" (2:9). Have you ever been faced with a severe physical condition? What was your response to God? Looking back on it, what were you able to learn and accomplish in the midst of the crisis?

8. Job reminds us that, along with physical needs, we also have emotional, relational, and spiritual needs. In the midst of his anguish, Job cries out to the Lord for understanding and vindication, especially against his three friends, who end up bringing more misery into his life. Spend some time going over what you

identified earlier in the chapter as your own emotional, relational, and spiritual needs. How would your
list have helped Job in his situation? How has your list
helped you in the past?

For those of you who haven't seen the movie *Cast Away* with
Tom Hanks, I'd like you to watch it this week. If you've already
seen it, consider seeing it again so you can view it in the context
of what we've just talked about.

After you've watched the movie, ask yourself these questions:

1. In my own life, who is my picture in the cave? (Who
gives me relationship?)

2. In my own life, what is my Wilson? (Who gives me
companionship?)

3. In my own life, what is my FedEx box? (What gives me
purpose?)

4. As I think of my own life, what is my sail? (What provides me a way to overcome obstacles?)

> *Father, I thank You for knowing my needs*
> *even when I don't. Give me the courage*
> *to examine my life and understand the*
> *truth about my priorities—about what*

my priorities are instead of what I want them to be. Grant me clear vision to discern the truth between my needs and wants. Help me have courage and not to be afraid.

2

Examine Your Excess

Now this is what the LORD Almighty says:
"Give careful thought to your ways. You have
planted much, but have harvested little. You
eat, but never have enough. You drink, but
never have your fill. You put on clothes, but
are not warm. You earn wages, only to put
them in a purse with holes in it." (Hag. 1:5–6)

It's been said about the stuff you find in garage sales that "one man's trash is another man's treasure." Conversely, that would mean that one man's treasure is another man's trash. Garage-sale treasures aside—is the same true for God-given treasures? Do we turn things that God intended as treasures into something less appealing? I believe we do; we take things that God intended for good and trash them or abuse them until that good pleasure becomes a prison.

Our "prison cells" are lush. They're cushioned with lots of our favorite foods and a well-stocked liquor or medicine cabinet. To drown out the sounds of true hunger, we fill them with all manner of noisy and absorbing distractions. The bars on our prison cells are made from the relationships we enter into and the possessions we purchase. We easily find ourselves imprisoned by those very things that are often no problem for someone else.

We each tend to harbor one or more secret activity or behavior that we just can't seem to get enough of. This "never enough" activity becomes our absolute necessity, our reward, our coping mechanism. We *need* (or so we think) this activity to insulate ourselves from the world. Because this world can be a pretty tough place, we need a lot of insulation.

In moderation and proper context, this "never enough" activity or behavior can even be a good thing. Problems arise when we think that a little of this feels good, so a lot should feel even better. But, as the verses from Haggai warn, it doesn't. This, however, doesn't stop us from trying—hard. Pretty soon, our "never enough" activity is the wheel in the cage, and we've become the rodent ... running and running and running but ultimately going nowhere.

SPINNING YOUR WHEELS

We're going to look at a montage of activities and behaviors I've seen used as someone's "never enough": food, alcohol, caffeine, electronics, work, shopping, tobacco, pharmaceuticals, exercise, hobbies, gambling, sex, relationships, money, anger, and guilt. You may have grimaced slightly at the mention of things in this list that appear either spot on or a distinct possibility for you or someone you love. A sigh of relief may have accompanied any you've already relegated to the "not me" category. Before you get too far ahead, I'll ask you to back up just a bit and really delve into each of these, attempting to withhold prejudgment.

Also, this is not an all-encompassing list. I've seen a great deal over the years, and one of the things I've observed is the ability for people to absolutely individualize their excessities. For some, your own particular brand of "never enough" didn't make my list. Is this because it isn't a legitimate "never enough"? No, it just means it didn't make my list—and perhaps there are even *echoes* of it swirling through others that did make it on the list. So open your mind to the rhythm of each of these, and see if you don't dance to a similar, if slightly variant, tune.

FOOD

A good deal of my work over the years has focused on eating disorders and what I've come to call "disordered eating." I've seen food become a "never enough" activity through an astonishing prism of personal angles. I've seen those of concentration-camp thinness who are so afraid of being fat they feel they can never become thin enough. I've seen morbidly obese people so emotionally tied to the food they consume that they eat and eat but never feel full. I've seen people who use food as a pleasure-punishment cycle in an all-encompassing ritual of binge, purge, and binge again until their teeth rot and their stomachs develop a nasty of habit of involuntary vomiting.

Granted, these are extremes, but I've also seen people who felt that virtually no food or drink was "safe" and that therefore any consumption was a fearful event. They might allow themselves to eat from a very small list of foods, but it is never done easily or without fear and remorse. I have regularly seen people who took food out of the box of nutrition and sprinkled it on all sorts of other things—loneliness, boredom, insecurity, anxiety, and fear. I've seen people with as intricate and involved a relationship with food as the most ardent of lovers.

What all of these people have in common is a specific perception of food and eating—one that is not based in reality. For them, food is not consumed to fill a nutritional need; rather, it is used to fill an emotional desire.

The human body needs a quantifiable amount of nutrients and energy to function at an optimum level. Vitamins, minerals, amino acids, fats, carbohydrates, proteins, and fiber all play their part. If food is appropriately consumed from a nutritional standpoint, it is possible to eat and be filled. When the hunger being fed is physical hunger, it is possible to have enough.

Not so with emotional hunger, which is notoriously difficult to identify, let alone fill. Unlike the stomach that signals fullness, emotional hunger can be a ravenous taskmaster. Because food is used as a surrogate to the real need, its effects are transitory at best. It is important to remember there are two ways that food can be used to fulfill emotional desires—food that is eaten and food that is restricted. Some people receive an emotional hit when food is eaten, and other people receive that same sense of satisfaction when food is denied.

All that being said, food is relatively convenient; it is there when other things are not and therefore especially susceptible to the *Gotta Have It!* impulse. It reminds me of the words to that old song by Stephen Stills: "If you can't be with the one you love, love the one you're with."[1] For too many people with unmet needs, they are resigned to food as the one they're with.

The preoccupation with food—what to eat, when to eat, where to eat, with whom to eat, how much to eat, how much to restrict, how much to indulge, how much to regret—sends up such a cloud of distraction that other pressing needs are simply pushed out of the way. Those pressing needs are often ones people do not wish to acknowledge because of the pain they produce. Distraction becomes a necessity, and food as a vehicle for that distraction is taken to excess. In this way, food becomes an excessity.

ALCOHOL

You've probably heard the term "drinking to excess." For many who drink to excess, the drinking becomes a necessity, which becomes an excessity. When confronted with the choice to either drink—and bear the negative consequences of their alcohol use—or stop, they will look longingly at that drink and say *Gotta Have It!*

The difficulty with alcohol is the penchant for denial and underestimating the amount of alcohol consumed. People do not begin drinking assuming they will become alcoholics. Rarely does a person voluntarily come into our facility for treatment with eyes opened wide about his or her alcohol use. More typically, something has caused them to get a chemical-dependency evaluation (which covers alcohol, illicit drugs, and prescription medications). Sometimes a DUI or alcohol-related arrest propels them through our doors in hopes of fulfilling a court requirement—right along with a personal determination not to have to give up their drinking.

With their families deserting them, their employment in jeopardy, their health deteriorating, and their hobbies reduced to a one-armed motion of hand to mouth, you would think that more people would recognize the problem alcohol has become in their lives. What starts out as a way to "have fun" or check out of life and its problems can quickly become something devastating. Either through conscious intent or genetic predisposition, alcohol use can fast-track to abuse and dependence.

When alcohol reaches the dependence stage, it is indeed a necessity—a physical one. Withdrawal from alcohol is unpleasant at best and life threatening at worst, depending upon the length and severity of the alcohol use, as well as a person's genetic and physical makeup. At this point, it's not just a matter of willpower; it's a matter of physical dependence. With prolonged and chronic alcohol use, withdrawal should be done in a medically supervised setting.

CAFFEINE

Perhaps you don't have an issue with alcohol. But what about caffeinated beverages? This includes coffee, flavored coffee drinks, certain teas, and caffeinated sodas. People who will hide their flask of liquor in the drawer of their desk won't think twice about their coffee consumption. If you were to take a poll of your friends, family, coworkers, and acquaintances, I think you'd find many more were attached to their latte than their liquor. In our society, caffeine is acceptable.

But what happens when your caffeine consumption takes on an exaggerated position in your life? I've seen people who didn't feel comfortable unless they carried around their lidded hot cup—a security blanket wrapped in a cardboard sleeve. I've seen people who experienced anxiety if told they needed to cut down on their caffeine consumption and were fearful of what that would mean. I've seen people who would rather give up food than this type of drink. They consume to excess, and their consumption is considered a necessity.

ELECTRONICS

Our next excessity comes in the form of electronics. By this I mean things like television, computers, the Internet, and computer-type games. It also includes all kinds of cell phones and iPods.

For some of you, I just crossed over a line. You're saying, "Wait a minute! I *need* my cell phone, and disaster will surely strike if I can't access my email!" In a confessional moment, I must admit that this category hits fairly close to home. I *love* all these gadgets! The days of driving without a portable GPS are a distant and good-riddance memory. The days of having to actually find a phone to make a call have been relegated to my own personal dustbin of history. The days of waiting for the morning paper or the evening news to know what's happening in the world seem archaic and restrictive. I simply cannot remember how I lived without electronics. The danger is when I start to believe I can't.

Electronics can fall into two camps—gadgets that help you stay connected and gadgets that help you disconnect. Both have their place in our lives. As Ecclesiastes 3:1 says, "There is a time for everything, and a season for every activity under heaven." There is a time to email and a time to refrain from emailing. There is a time to turn on the television and a time to turn it off. There is a time to be online and a time to be off-line. Since none of us have the wisdom of Solomon, how do we know when that is?

I have worked with people who experience unease, discomfort, and anxiousness if they are not able to stay digitally connected to the world or their work (which to some are the same thing). If they are out for an evening with family or friends, they'll steal away in private to check their email on their BlackBerry. When they should be in bed asleep, they are instead blurry eyed in front of the computer screen. For these people there is no such thing as "downtime." They experience a sense of dread and a premonition of disaster if they stay too long without knowing exactly what's going on in their corner of cyberspace.

I have also worked with people who consistently choose the mind-numbing effect of television, the computer, and all manner of games to escape the problems and the perils of the real world. Zoning out in front of the television is nothing new. However, when observing life becomes more important than living it, there's a problem. When existing in cyberspace becomes more compelling than living life in the real world, there's also a problem.

In some ways, electronic gaming combines the power of both the television and the computer. With games, you have the visual punch and emotional story line of television along with the command and control features of the computer. With gaming, you become the story line. When your avatars, alter egos, and digital doppelgängers are more present, more real, more engaging than anything real time has to offer, there's a problem.

WORK

How can working be considered a bad thing? What's wrong with working hard and trying to do your best? I usually hear these questions when people come to realize they've spent the last weeks (or months, years, or decades) building their careers while at the same time destroying their relationships.

Work and the achievement it brings can definitely be put on a good list unless it takes away from other good things. When does doing something good turn into doing something bad? This is not always an easy line to determine. It is the line between working and being a workaholic. It is the line between doing something good because it is good and doing something good because it feels good to you but really isn't.

Jesus brought up this concept earlier in Matthew 6:5. He's talking about the Pharisees, the religiously pious of that day, who would go to the synagogues and street corners to pray. You'd think Jesus would applaud prayer, but that's not the case here. In this case Jesus wasn't so much interested in what they were doing, but why they were doing it. Were they praying? Yes, but their motivation was not to converse with God; it was to be seen by others. Good action but lousy reason. There are all kinds of rewards for working hard. The problem comes when those rewards are considered more valuable than other positives in your life, like your health, your emotional well-being, and your relationships.

SHOPPING

For some people, shopping is arduous work. Just ask me how much I like going to the mall a week before Christmas. For others, shopping is pure pleasure, so much so that making a purchase elicits the same physical reaction as a lover's caress or a hot fudge sundae. Remember Imelda Marcos's shoes? I would guess she experienced a burst of pleasure every time she bought another pair.

Shopping can be a way of escaping the tedium of reality. Whether it's the latest electronic gadget or clothing style or hobby hardware, each purchase comes with a whispered promise: Your life somehow will be better once you have whatever it is. Often, it is. However, shopping becomes an excessity when you feel compelled to shop even when you don't really have the time, the money, or the need for the things you buy. It becomes an excessity when you've run out of things to buy for yourself—and room to store all that stuff—and begin to purchase things for friends and family without being asked or encouraged. It's an excessity when you feel deprived, depressed, or anxious when prevented from shopping. When the mall is the only place you really feel at home and in control, there's a problem.

TOBACCO

The nicotine in tobacco products is an addictive substance. It alters your body chemistry so that you're different with it than you are without it. Without it, you can become irritable, anxious, hostile, depressed, impatient, and restless. Smoking, with its physical effects, is definitely a *Gotta Have It!* activity. But tobacco isn't just smoked; it's also snorted, dipped, and chewed. Whatever its form, tobacco has nicotine as a powerful, addictive hook.

PHARMACEUTICALS

I'm glad to live in a time when understanding and research have advanced to the point where so many chronic conditions and symptoms can be relieved or even eliminated through the use of pharmaceutical medications. These pharmaceuticals are like a two-sided coin—each has its positive, beneficial side and its negative, harmful side. If something is strong enough to help you, it's also probably strong enough to harm you if not used properly.

The National Institute on Drug Abuse (NIDA) says the following: "The nonmedical use or abuse of prescription drugs is a serious and growing health problem in this country."[2] Abuse comes when these wonder drugs are used outside of their narrowly defined prescribed-use parameters. Any prescription drug has the potential for abuse, but there are certain categories that appear more at risk. NIDA identifies the following: "Commonly abused classes of prescription medications include opioids (for pain), central nervous system depressants (for anxiety and sleep disorders), and stimulants (for ADHD and narcolepsy)."[3] According to the same report, "In 2008, 15.2 million American age 12 and older had taken a prescription pain reliever, tranquilizer, stimulant, or sedative for nonmedical purposes at least once in the year prior to being surveyed."[4]

This study was based upon prescribed medications and did not even investigate the abuse that goes on with over-the-counter products and medications, such as sleeping aids, laxatives, and appetite suppressants. When dealing with these substances, a little may be good, but a lot is definitely not.

EXERCISE

Some of you will look at this category and wonder how in the world it ever made it onto the list. Others of you will cringe and wish it could somehow disappear. The first group is made up of those for whom exercise is a foreign, distasteful concept. The latter group is made up of those for whom exercise is an excessity, an absolute way of life.

Please don't misunderstand—I think regular exercise should be part of everyone's lifestyle, in whatever form is appropriate for your current condition and situation. I know it is for me. I enjoy exercise, and it enhances my life and my health. There are also days when, honestly, it's the last thing I really want to do.

Exercise becomes an excessity when its position on your priority scale is so high that you'll forgo just about everything else in order to do it. You'll exercise when sick or injured. You'll exercise even if it interferes with other responsibilities, including family obligations. Exercise is an excessity when it becomes too tightly tied to your feelings of self-esteem, when you feel anxious, guilty, and irritable if you don't exercise. When it becomes a source of inordinate pride and self-identification, it's a problem.

HOBBIES

The word *hobby* seems so innocuous. How harmful can hobbies be? Aren't they supposed to be your leisure-time activities? Hobbies, however, by their very nature, have the propensity to become excessities because they are one of the few activities during your day or week that you specifically choose to do. Everyone has to sleep, and most people have to work. Put those two activities together, and you get roughly two-thirds of your weekdays spoken for. Add in preparation time, travel time, running errands, and other responsibilities, and you find you have a small window of discretionary time for doing what you want. This is the sliver of time hobbies fit into.

But what happens when those hobbies don't quite fit into that sliver of time? What happens when they're so much fun, so rewarding, or so pleasurable that they start to expand and ooze out of that small window? Something else has to give. When that something else is work, sleep, or family responsibilities, that harmless hobby has turned into a monster.

GAMBLING

I wrote a whole book about this particular excessity some years ago.[5] I continue to be surprised at how few resources are available for those struggling with compulsive gambling.

For those hooked, gambling is not a harmless hobby. It is not a night at the casino twice a year with friends or the monthly poker get-together with the crowd from work and a three-raise, quarter limit. It's not a yearly trip to Vegas with your high school buddies, mostly for the shows. For those hooked, gambling is a serious activity; it is the exhilaration of the win and the agony of the loss. It is the promise of an end to all your problems or at least a temporary reprieve. It is the one activity where your desire and need to win somehow seem strong enough to bend the laws of chance and physics. When gambling reaches this level, it isn't about fun; it's about faith: the faith that with this race, this game, this throw, this hand—this time—the world will right itself, and you'll win once again.

SEX

If pleasure has the ability to turn activities into excessities, it's not difficult to understand how sexual activity could become one. When sex becomes an excessity, fulfilling that desire is all-encompassing. I've seen couples married for decades blown apart when sex with someone else becomes more important than the marriage. I've seen devastation wrought on families when sexual desire is hijacked by pornography over the Internet. I've seen the pain and humiliation when one person's sexual proclivities become paramount in the sexual relationship. I've watched the tears and recriminations, the anger and blame, hurled by couples at each other with lethal force, bringing about the death of relationship—all over sex. I've seen the act God intended to enhance intimacy and love used to sow discord and distance, tearing apart relationships.

Sex becomes an excessity when what you want becomes more important than what God wants, what your spouse wants, or what you need. If you throw caution to the wind where sex is concerned and adopt a whatever-feels-good mentality, there's a storm brewing in your life, if it hasn't hit already.

RELATIONSHIPS

Relationship excessities aren't always of a sexual nature. Sometimes, the excessity relationship I see is between parent and child. It is a disturbing distortion of the natural bonding that should occur, where one appears unable to detach and function without the other. *Bonding* becomes *bondage*. This kind of enmeshment between mother and daughter often manifests itself in an eating disorder—the daughter's symptom of the mother's relational stranglehold. I have also seen it in oppositional defiant disorder between a father and son, where the son assumes a constant position of hostility in order to avoid the suffocation of his father's need for control over his life.

Relationships can also become an excessity when it is the fact of the relationship, not the face of the relationship, that matters most. I've seen people jump from relationship to relationship, refusing to grow and learn from each, in order to perpetuate a deep-seated pattern. For these people, the faces change but the circumstances do not. He's forever looking for someone who needs him so much she'll be afraid to leave. She's forever looking for someone who is wounded more than she is so her hurt won't seem so bad. I've seen people who needed to be in a relationship so badly—who could not tolerate being alone—they compromised just about everything. If you keep looking in the mirror when it comes to relationships and say to yourself over and over, "I can't believe I keep doing this!" it's time to determine if being in relationship has become an excessity in your life.

MONEY

Money is a huge "never enough" for many people—and not just for our current materialistic culture. It was also an issue back in King Solomon's day; he notes the following in his book outlining his search for wisdom and meaning in life: "Whoever loves money never has money enough; whoever loves wealth is never satisfied with his income. This too is meaningless" (Eccl. 5:10).

Clearly, it's possible to be head over heels in love with money. Jesus put it pretty bluntly when He said, "No one can serve two masters. Either he will hate the one and love the other, or he will be devoted to the one and despise the other. You cannot serve both God and Money" (Matt. 6:24). The writer of Hebrews warns, "Keep your lives free from the love of money and be content with what you have" (Heb. 13:5a). When you fail to heed this warning, money has the potential to become a powerful "never enough" in your life.

But is it really the jingle of coins or the snap of a crisp dollar bill that's so gratifying? Is it money itself or what money represents that's so compelling? In my experience, money is just an avenue to power and control. Power and control are heady commodities, as seductive and addictive in their own ways as the most potent of drugs. Money is the conduit through which power and control flow. It's been that way since Solomon's time.

Just a word of clarification: You don't have to be wealthy to be a lover of money. Nowhere in Scripture does it say it is only the wealthy who love money. First Timothy 6:10 says, "For the love of money is a root of all kinds of evil. Some people, eager for money, have wandered from the faith and pierced themselves with many griefs." It is the *attitude*—not the *amount*—that is important. As you consider whether or not money is an excessity in your life, the answer will more likely lie in your heart than in your bank ledger.

ANGER

Some of you are probably scrunching up your eyebrows at this category. After all, who would *want* to gather up and surround themselves with an excessity of anger? Yet for some people, each expression of anger is as precious to them—to their sense of self and identification in the world—as Imelda Marcos's espadrilles were to her. Just as Imelda felt more herself and more complete with every pair of shoes, there are some people who intentionally "put on" anger every day as a personal statement and protective covering.

You probably know someone like this. It's the person who is able to find fault in just about every person she meets and every situation she encounters. Nothing is left alone to be just what it is. It is always critiqued, criticized, evaluated, and ultimately found lacking. She reacts the same way to people. Coworkers are incompetent; her kids are a mess, her husband (or ex-husband) a fool. She considers herself akin to the only sighted person in the land of the blind, constantly amazed at the ineptitude around her. Therefore, she feels duty bound to continually, incessantly point it out. It is impossible for her to leave well enough alone because, to her, it's never well enough; the only "well enough" is her "never enough"—her anger, irritation, and annoyance. For her, living out her wellspring of anger every day is a necessity for her sense of self and as a defensive stance against a hostile world. Yes, her anger is an excessity.

This isn't an issue just for women; men also can exhibit inappropriate levels of anger. It's the man who doesn't speak to others as much as he barks at them. Questions and comments are really thinly veiled commands. He always has an opinion, is never afraid to voice it, and rarely has one that is positive. This is the man who attacks life from the position of an adversary. He is convinced that people are out to get him and that only eternal vigilance on his part—sometimes expressed in a raised and animated voice—keeps him and his family safe. His family has learned not to question him, and the dog wisely stays out of his way.

Like money, anger is a conduit for power and control. Anger is *effective*. Angry people usually get what they want through the feelings their anger generates in others. Most people are afraid of angry people and will attempt to accommodate them or placate them. Usually this means giving up something to the person who is angry, even if what is given up is the other person's self-control. Yes, anger is effective and powerful. Because of this, anger has the potential to crowd out other responses in your emotional toolbox until it's the first thing you reach for, every time.

GUILT

In my twenty-five years of counseling others, I've seen guilt pulled out and put on just about as often as anger. It can be much quieter, though, especially when a person wears the guilt instead of placing it onto someone else. Guilt, when thrown over others, has the potential to be noisily, loudly, angrily rejected and shaken off. Guilt, when worn by the person, however, is generally quiet, like a shroud. Whereas anger is retaliatory, guilt is preemptive. Guilt says, *You don't need to hurt me; I'll do it myself.* By administering a self-inflicted blow, guilt seeks to control the level—if not the presence—of pain. Guilt is a way to make yourself responsible for and thus in control of the pain in your life. The guiltier you feel, the more pain you experience. The more pain you experience, the more apt you are to attempt to control it through guilt. This is what leads to guilt becoming an excessity for some.

Planting Seeds

It's time to go back over the list and do some digging around to examine if and how much each behavior has become an excessity in your life. This isn't an easy or comfortable thing to do. It is, however, essential. By understanding *what* your "never enoughs" are, you can begin to uncover *why* they're never enough.

This isn't some sort of test, where you want to skew the results to make yourself look good. Be honest and open with yourself. Don't necessarily write down the first thing that comes to your mind. Really think over your answers, and work through them until you know they reflect the truth. Each excessity covers up a need in your life. You can't get to your real needs until you go through the process to uncover the truth. It's okay to be apprehensive.

The questions below are generally yes/no questions. Try to avoid middle ground or an "I don't know" response. If you can answer yes in any way, be specific about when and why that is.

For most of you, you're going to need more room for your answers than what is provided here, so feel free to use other paper or a notebook.

I heartily suggest you make this a prayerful exercise and pray prior to beginning, at any point you feel called during this exercise, and after you are done. You are engaging in an exercise of discernment regarding yourself and your life, and wisdom is a valuable tool. It is a perverse characteristic of human beings that we are notoriously obtuse when it comes to being wise about ourselves. Often, we simply need someone else to help us navigate the twists and turns of our own excuses, rationalizations, blind spots, and justifications. That brings me to this promise from James 1:5: "If any of you lacks wisdom, he should ask God, who gives generously to all without finding fault, and it will be given to him." It is God's desire to give you wisdom and discernment in completing this exercise.

FOOD

Do you often find yourself eating when you're not really hungry?

Do you sometimes continue to eat to the point of physical discomfort?

Do you regularly feel guilty after you eat?

Do you think about food continually during the day, worrying about what you'll eat, when you'll eat, and how much you'll eat?

Are you dissatisfied with your body, how much you weigh, and how you look?

ALCOHOL

Have you ever felt you should cut down on your drinking?

Have you ever been annoyed when people questioned your drinking?

Have you ever felt guilty about your drinking?

Have you ever needed a drink in the morning as a way to wake up and feel "normal"?

CAFFEINE

Do you need a cup of coffee or a caffeinated drink in the morning to really get going?

Have you ever felt jittery or restless during the day?

Do you drink coffee or caffeinated drinks during the day to keep alert and fight off becoming sleepy?

Does your use of caffeine interfere with your ability to go to sleep at night?

ELECTRONICS

Do you find yourself anxious or nervous unless you have access to your cell phone or computer?

Do you regularly spend more time than you planned accessing electronic devices, either to keep up with messages or to play games?

When you have a choice to be with people or be online, do you find you more often choose the latter?

Has anyone questioned you about how much time you're spending either online or connected to your cell phone, iPod, or other electronic device?

Would you have difficulty being separated from all electronic devices for more than a day?

WORK

Do you get more excited about your work than about family or anything else?

Do you take your work with you to bed? On weekends? On vacation?

Have your family members or friends given up expecting you to be on time?

Do you believe it is okay to work long hours if you love what you are doing?

Do you get irritated when people ask you to stop doing your work in order to do something else?[6]

SHOPPING

Do you regularly spend more when shopping than you mean to?

Do you buy multiple items when you only really need one or two?

Do you hide your purchases or your receipts?

Do you often take back the things you purchase?

Would you rather go shopping than do just about any other activity?

TOBACCO

Do you need to smoke every day to feel good?

Have you seriously attempted to quit one or more times but been unsuccessful?

Do you experience moodiness and irritability if you can't smoke or use tobacco?

Do you keep smoking even though your family has asked or your doctor has told you to stop?

Will you avoid going out with friends or family if it is to a place that is designated as nonsmoking?

PHARMACEUTICALS

Do you regularly take more of your prescription medication than directed by your physician?

Have you ever altered a prescription or gone to more than one physician in order to obtain more of the medication?

Do you take the pills now just to feel "normal"?

Do you conceal from family, friends, and your physician the amount of medication you're taking?

EXERCISE

Do you exercise more than six days a week?

Do you become irritable if you're not able to exercise for more than a few days?

Do you continue to exercise even if you're significantly injured and in pain?

Do you become annoyed if someone asks you to do something that interferes with your ability to exercise, even for a single day?

HOBBIES

Do you regularly shave time off work or with family in order to engage in your hobby?

Have family members ever talked to you about how much time you're spending on your hobby?

Do you regularly find you spend more time on your hobby than you originally intended?

Do you spend more money than you're really able to in order to support your hobby?

GAMBLING

Do you ever lose time from school or work because of gambling?

Has gambling ever made your home life unhappy?

Have you ever felt remorse after gambling?

After losing do you ever feel you must return as soon as possible and win back your losses?

Are you reluctant to use your "gambling money" for normal expenditures?[7]

SEX

Do you keep secrets about your sexual or romantic activities from those close to you?

Do you lead a double life?

Have your needs driven you to have sex in places or situations or with people you would not normally chose?

Do you find yourself looking for sexually arousing materials in newspapers, magazines, or online?

Is it taking more variety and frequency of sexual and romantic activities than previously to bring about the same levels of excitement and relief?

Does your pursuit of sex or romantic relationships interfere with your spiritual beliefs or development?[8]

RELATIONSHIPS

Do you find yourself repeating patterns in relationships?

Do you find yourself uncomfortable or anxious if you are not in a relationship?

Do you derive a sense of identity and pride from your relationships?

Is it important for you to be in control of the people you are in relationship with?

Do you find yourself living vicariously through the people you are in relationship with?

MONEY

Do you regularly spend time thinking about how to make more money?

Do you often dream about what you would do if you won the lottery or received a large amount of cash?

Do you calculate your value based upon the amount of the money you make?

Have you ever lied or cheated in order to make or keep money?

Have you ever resented spending money on others instead of being able to keep it for yourself?

ANGER

Have family members or friends ever questioned you about your temper?

Do you find that you are often irritated, annoyed, or frustrated over other people, circumstances, or life in general?

Do you often critique or criticize other people or situations?

Do you feel more empowered or emboldened when you are angry?

Do you regularly regret things you say when you're angry?

GUILT

Do you regularly think about things in your past that you are ashamed of?

When something goes wrong around you, do you assume
    you're somehow at fault?

Do you regularly feel the need to apologize to other
    people?

Do you regularly defer to others even when you don't
    really want to?

Are you fearful of telling other people no?

You've probably figured out that the more times you say yes
to these questions, the greater the potential for a category to be
an excessity in your life. I'm not going to tell you that if you *only*
answered one or two in each category with a yes that there isn't
something to be worked on and worked through. Actually, only
you can determine how much of an issue each of these is to your
life. Even answering yes to one or two in any of these categories
can indicate an open door for an excessity to come barging in at
some point.

However, please don't be overly alarmed if you recognize
an issue with several of these categories. Excessities tend
to run in packs. In counseling jargon they are called "co-
occurring." Take heart; several may be connected together
through a single root need. When you identify and address
the root, you'll be able to make progress on more than one
category. That's what we're going to tackle next—coming to
an understanding of your true needs that have been masked

by your excessities. Unmask and meet the need, and the power of the excessity diminishes.

> *Lord, I ask for a clarity of sight, courage of heart, and peace of mind as I take a deep look into behaviors, patterns, and habits that have too strong an influence in my life. As the Serenity Prayer says, grant me the courage to do what is necessary in order to change. I confess I am afraid of the power these things have over my life, and I purposefully entrust my fear to You. Hold me close when I am afraid and let me feel Your presence to give me courage. Thank You for the gift of wisdom. Thank You also for not finding fault with me because of my lack of wisdom. Thank You for Your generosity to me.*

Section 2

Our True Needs

Coal miners used to carry canaries with them down into the mine shafts. These birds served a valuable purpose. If dangerous gases such as carbon monoxide or methane became present in the tunnels, the gases would kill the canaries first, signaling the coal miners to evacuate immediately. The birds acted as a warning system, alerting the miners to danger.

In a way, that's what you've done through the last chapter. You've put your canaries in a cage as you've identified your excessities. These excessities act as a warning system, alerting you of unmet needs, because whenever you engage in an excessity, there is a true need at the core of that behavior.

Needs are not bad. We have a need for air, for food, for shelter, for companionship. We have a God-designed need for the divine in our lives. Our problems come from how we choose to fill those needs. Our problems come when our wants, our preferences, our choices, our excessities supersede and obscure our true needs. Though we desperately think otherwise, the former are inadequate to fill the latter.

God, as our loving Father, understands our needs, as Jesus reassures us in the Sermon on the Mount (Matt. 6:31–33). Our challenge is to learn how to meet our true needs without engaging in our excessities.

3

Our Need for Comfort

The idols speak deceit, diviners see visions
that lie; they tell dreams that are false,
they give comfort in vain. Therefore the
people wander like sheep oppressed
for lack of a shepherd. (Zech. 10:2)

We still live in a harsh world with deceit, lies, and falsehoods—a world where one of our deepest needs is to be comforted, but that comfort is often in vain. Just like the people in Zechariah's day, we seek comfort in all the wrong places. Any comfort received from these false sources is fleeting at best, requiring us to continue in fruitless comfort-seeking behavior.

JENNIFER'S STORY

Jennifer needed comfort every day. When she prayed, "Give us this day our daily bread," she meant it for comfort, not for food. Bread—in all its carbohydrate forms—was Jennifer's comforter. She liked just about anything baked, but there was something sublime about fresh, hot, yeasty bread with its crusty, crunchy outside and soft, warm middle. And when it was slathered with sweet and salty butter … well, there just wasn't anything more comforting to Jennifer. Often, she would go to the market near her house specifically to buy a fresh loaf of French bread, knowing just what time the hot loaves would be set out on the racks by the checkout stand. Before she got the bread home, along with the other groceries she bought as cover, she would eat over half the loaf, tearing off large pieces, gulping them down in the front seat like someone winded gulps for air.

Life made Jennifer feel winded—physically, emotionally, and spiritually. Food—bread in particular—helped to ease that discomfort and give Jennifer a sense of relief. Lost within that moment of fulfillment, Jennifer felt a golden sense of being satisfied, something she rarely felt during her life-as-usual.

The only problem for Jennifer was that fulfillment never lasted very long. By the time she got the bread home and put away the rest of the groceries, it was already starting to cool off, and the kids wanted in on the action. Before she knew it, the loaf was gone along with that transcendent moment of relief. Instead, it was replaced by anxiety over her weight and how much she'd eaten. Everything about the bread, it seemed, always went from warm to cold.

COMFORT FOOD

Food is a comfort commodity. From our earliest moments of life outside the womb, one of our first feelings of distress and discomfort comes from hunger. And one of our first feelings of being comforted comes from being fed. There were panic and agitation;

then there were relief and calming. Growing up, you may have lived in a household where food was given as a universal pacifier. When you were hungry, you were fed. When you were upset, you were fed. When you were bored, you were fed. When you were good, you were fed. When there was reason for celebration, you were fed. You may have grown up in a home where the best conduit for love and comfort came directly through the kitchen. And the feeling of being loved rode in on the aroma of something good coming from the oven or the stove.

Or you could have grown up in a home where real connection was tenuous and comfort a do-it-yourself proposition. In the absence of any affectionate feelings or expressed love, you learned that the comfort found in food was ultimately more reliable and always more controllable. You learned to grab comfort where you could because at your house it was in chronically short supply.

Often, because of denials and rationalizations, it can be difficult to reach an understanding of how much a role food plays in comfort seeking. People tend to downplay the need for their food of choice; they downplay the amount they actually consume of it; they downplay the importance it has appropriated in their lives. They downplay all of these things until they are asked to withhold that food of choice. When this happens, they quickly realize it has become their go-to source of comfort.

When speaking of comfort, food is the first thing that comes to my mind because of the amount of eating disorders I work with, but I have seen many other activities join the go-to-for-comfort club. I have seen that loaf of French bread replaced by a double-tall caramel macchiato. I have seen that double-tall caramel macchiato

replaced by a video game controller. I have seen that game controller replaced by a credit card. I have seen that credit card replaced by
the satisfaction of a verbal outburst or a sarcastic put-down. The ways
people choose to provide themselves with comfort is virtually endless. When you factor in each person's unique situation and capacity
for creativity, the permutations go off the chart.

THE NATURE OF COMFORT AND DISCOMFORT

I believe an answer to taming these comfort-seeking excessities is
to understand the nature of comfort and its flip side of discomfort. Comfort is something that produces relief, encouragement,
contentment, satisfaction, or enjoyment. Discomfort produces
distress and unease. These are internal feelings. They may be
produced by external circumstances, but it is our individual inter-
pretation that determines whether those circumstances bring us
comfort or discomfort. One person's comfort is another person's
distress. A job promotion for one person may produce feelings
of encouragement and satisfaction, while the same promotion for
another person may produce feelings of fear and uncertainty. A
three-course meal may produce feelings of contentment in one
person, while the same three-course meal may produce feelings
of extreme unease in someone else. This is why it's not enough
to determine the circumstances; you must also examine *how you
interpret* those circumstances. Interpretations of circumstances are
often influenced by a person's needs.

In the last chapter, you examined your excessities. In this chapter, I'd like you to think about what causes you either comfort or

discomfort. Sometimes, excessities are used to produce comfort—while at other times they are used to distract from discomfort. So it's not enough to just look at what you do to provide yourself comfort. You also need to examine what you do to distract yourself from feeling uncomfortable. How you view both comfort and discomfort becomes very important.

THE PRINCESS AND THE PEA

Comfort is highly prized in our culture, while discomfort is barely tolerated. I think of all of the ways we have to make our lives comfortable, from the houses we live in to the cars we drive. We buy comfortable clothes and comfortable shoes. Whenever possible our homes and work spaces are kept at a comfortable temperature. We have comfortable places to sit and comfortable places to sleep. Because we are surrounded by comfort, we have finely tuned radar for anything that causes us even a modicum of discomfort. For some of us, we have become the princess in that fable of *The Princess and the Pea*—the classic fairy tale of the princess who goes to bed on twenty feather beds atop twenty mattresses, under which the queen has place a single pea. In the morning, the princess says she was hardly able to sleep at all because of something hard in the bed and claims to be black and blue because of it. From this, the queen knows she is a real princess because no one else could be that sensitive.

I sometimes wonder if some of us have become the princess, and any discomfort—even caused by something as small and insignificant as a pea—is reason for an endless stream of complaint. While hypersensitivity is a virtue in this fairy tale, I'm not sure it plays out that well in real life because the greater your sensitivity to discomfort, the greater your need for relief. The greater your need for relief, the more susceptible you are to comfort-seeking excessities.

There are quite a few conditions that produce distress and unease. There are loneliness, anxiety, fear, guilt, boredom, and restlessness. There are irritation, frustration, and agitation. I have heard each of these given as a reason why people run to their particular excessity. They seek comfort from the distress and unease—the discomfort they feel has interrupted their lives, their sleep, their peace of mind—that have left them figuratively black and blue. They want relief, and they want it now.

But is that really the role of comfort? Is comfort meant to be a universal and immediate panacea for every uneasy thought or interpreted distress? When I was a new father, I thought my job was to rush in to comfort my child at the slightest sign of distress. It was difficult for me to hear him cry. I wanted to do something. Wisely, my wife reminded me that sometimes the best something to do is nothing. Children often are fussy and irritable "just because." They need to learn how to work through those feelings on their own. Sticking a pacifier or a bottle in their mouths or picking them up at every turn or giving in to every demand does not teach children to be adaptable; it teaches them to be dependent. It teaches a child that comfort comes from *outside*, instead of from within.

When children are young, they are dependent on adults for just about everything. As they get older, however, they begin to learn how to handle some of their needs. This fosters their sense of independence and identity. By letting children gradually learn how to handle their discomfort, they will grow and mature, learning how to weather the inevitable storms of life without looking for the quickest or most convenient way out. They will learn better how to weather distress and discomfort. This gives children the gift of resiliency. The more resilient they are, the less likely they are to reach for excessities.

Please do not mistake me here. I am not advocating depriving children of comfort. Far from it! For I have also seen what happens when comfort is chronically denied a child. Each occasion of distress and unease is geometrically heightened by the failure to comfort the time before. Panic and anxiety set in, producing a world where there is no minor discomfort because every discomfort is sucked into that black hole of neglect. When an excessity is grabbed on to in order to counterbalance that black hole, there isn't enough *Gotta Have It!* activity possible to fill the gap.

Each end of the spectrum produces an excessive response. Grow up with too much comfort from the outside, and we develop intolerance to any discomfort or an inability to generate comfort from the inside. Grow up with too little comfort, and we develop an insatiable need to fill that void.

DESENSITIZATION

I'd first like to look at what happens when you've become hypersensitized to discomfort. Maybe you grew up in a household where you barely had time to verbalize some perceived distress before something was shoved in your face—literally or figuratively—from food to clothes to things in general. Your ability to be patient was artificially stunted. It's no wonder you turn to any number of activities to make you feel better, because you lack perseverance muscles. Perhaps, for you, the best thing isn't to figure out a way to provide more comfort in your life, but rather to find a way to tolerate a little more of the normal discomfort life throws at you. This is desensitization.

Desensitization is defined as an intentional treatment that uses exposure to "emotionally distressing stimuli" in a graduated form. You start out small (small like a pea) and work your way up to handling more difficult situations. I've used this method with people who struggle with agoraphobia—literally "fear of the marketplace"—who are unable to leave their homes. Providing support, you begin to help the person conquer small challenges, such as going outside to get his mail or even just walking to the end of his driveway. Gradually, over time, you work up to walking around the block and taking short trips in the car. It is a deliberate strategy of walking alongside a person, addressing his fears, and assisting him to work through those fears, gaining success at learning how to overcome them.

ALLERGIC REACTION

It's interesting to me that desensitization is used not only in the treatment of mental health conditions but also in the medical treatment of allergens. It's almost as if we've become *allergic* to discomfort. Maybe you have hay fever. This means you're allergic to ordinary stuff like dust and pollen. These aren't things that will kill you, but you'd never know by your body's reaction. Your eyes swell up and tear in order to flush the allergen out. You sniffle and sneeze in an effort to expel the invader from your body. Your entire immune system goes on red alert over an inert substance that really isn't a threat at all. In fact, the person next to you can smell the flowers and simply enjoy them instead of going into a wheezing, sneezing, coughing fit.

Excessities can be kind of like that—they are an emotionally driven wheezing, sneezing, coughing fit, attempting to thwart an everyday, normal discomfort. If you are the type of person who is allergic to discomfort, you're probably the type of person who is susceptible to excessities.

People who benefit from desensitization are those who experience an extreme reaction to an everyday occurrence. Discomfort, in this life, is an everyday occurrence. From the time you wake up in the morning—even having to wake up, for me, on some days—to the time you go to sleep at night, there will always be something to cause you discomfort, if you look for it. Just like dust and pollen exist everywhere in our environment, so does discomfort. It's part of life.

THE ROLE OF COMFORT

Up to this point, we've really focused on the role of discomfort because discomfort causes us to engage in comfort-seeking behaviors. We have come to believe we should be comforted in any and all situations. If we are bored, lonely, angry, frustrated, fearful—you name it—we need to be comforted.

But what, really, is the role of comfort? Remember, we explained comfort as that which produces strengthening, consolation, relief, encouragement, contentment, satisfaction, or enjoyment. This is the world's definition of comfort, but what does God—the originator of comfort, the God of all comfort—say the role of comfort is in our lives?

In the New International Version of the Bible, the word *comfort* appears seventy-two times. Interestingly enough, the word *discomfort* only appears once. In Jonah 4:6, it says, "Then the LORD God provided a vine and made it grow up over Jonah to give shade for his head to ease his discomfort, and Jonah was very happy about the vine."

Two things to note in this verse: One, it says "ease his discomfort" not eradicate it; and, two, even easing discomfort can produce feelings of happiness. Yet, ease from discomfort is fleeting—as evidenced in the very next verse, when God causes a worm to come and chew the vine and kill it, leaving Jonah out of shade and back in discomfort. God uses this whole discomfort-vine-worm scenario to teach Jonah something about himself. When God took away the vine, which was so comforting to Jonah, Jonah became very angry. God used this as a way to show Jonah his misplaced priorities. Jonah was very concerned about the vine and about his own comfort. He was more concerned, in fact, about his own physical condition than he was about the spiritual condition of 120,000 souls in the city of Nineveh. Jonah, refusing to do what God wanted, rushed into the desert to pout and wound up angry because the desert is a place where there is little food, little water, little vegetation, and a whole lot of sun. Perhaps some of the discomfort we find in our own lives comes not from some worldly conspiracy against us but from the natural consequence of our own decisions. Like with Jonah, God may use our discomfort to teach us how to make better decisions next time and avoid that particular discomfort in the future.

Don't worry; we're not going to go in depth on each one of the seventy-two "comfort" verses, but there are a couple of general points

to be gleaned from looking at them as a whole. The first is there
is real need for comfort in life. *Comfort* can sometimes seem like
a fuzzy, feel-good, but lightweight kind of word, and maybe that's
because we've come to use it for things that are the equivalent of a
child needing comfort after stubbing a toe. According to Scripture,
there is a real need for comfort in life because there is real pain in life.
Here are a couple of examples where comfort is needed:

Because of a hard life of work and toil (Gen. 5:29)

Because of the death of a loved one (Gen. 24:67
and many others)

Because of prejudice and oppression (Ruth 2:13;
Eccl. 4:1)

Because of physical illness (Job 7:13)

Because of catastrophic life circumstances (Ps. 23:4;
Isa. 51:19)

Because of a broken heart (Ps. 69:20; Jer. 8:18)

Because of suffering (Ps. 119:50)

These are not lightweight circumstances. If comfort is designed
by God to combat situations such as these, it is obviously powerful.
If it is so powerful, why do so many people find it in such short

supply in their lives? And finding it in such short supply, why do so many people turn to so many things in an attempt to produce it? If you constantly reach out and say *Gotta Have It!* in an attempt to produce comfort in your life, these are very important questions.

In order to find your own personal answer, I'd like you to consider the following: Could it be that you have become hypersensitized to discomfort and desensitized to comfort by the activities you engage in? In other words, because so many things cause you discomfort and you run to all your excessities to provide comfort, you've forgotten what true comfort is really meant for. True comfort has gotten covered over with all of your fix-it-now, do-it-my-way excessities. True comfort comes from God; that is also abundantly clear in many of those seventy-two passages. If you've crowned yourself judge of your discomfort and king of your comfort, what role is there left for God? What if the way He wants to give you comfort doesn't match the pattern of your excessities? Which one will you choose?

Could it be that your excessities and the fleeting comfort they bring are covering up the real reason why you need true comfort?

These are not easy questions to answer, but they are vital questions to discover the answer to if you are serious about understanding your reactions. Comfort—both true and false—lies at the heart of your behavior. Comfort also lies at the heart of God Himself. He is the originator of comfort, knowing and understanding the pain and suffering that have come into this world. That was never His plan, but comfort—true comfort—is one of His solutions.

His plan is found in 2 Corinthians 1:3–7, in which the word *comfort* is used nine times:

> Praise be to the God and Father of our Lord
> Jesus Christ, the Father of compassion and
> the God of all comfort, who comforts us
> in all our troubles, so that we can comfort
> those in any trouble with the comfort we
> ourselves have received from God. For just
> as the sufferings of Christ flow over into our
> lives, so also through Christ our comfort
> overflows. If we are distressed, it is for your
> comfort and salvation; if we are comforted,
> it is for your comfort, which produces in
> you patient endurance of the same suf-
> ferings we suffer. And our hope for you is
> firm, because we know that just as you share
> in our sufferings, so also you share in our
> comfort.

Do you notice here how many times comfort and suffering are
linked together? Did you notice how comfort is a circular affair? One
person suffers and God provides comfort. With that comfort, the
person who suffers is both comforted and able to comfort. I will tell
you honestly that some of the suffering of others I have observed over
the years makes no sense to me at all. I cannot find any reason for it,
and it has at times stretched my belief in a caring and compassion-
ate God. But so often I have been comforted in that doubt by the
very people who suffered so. It's nothing short of miraculous—those
people are able to find comfort in that horrific suffering by providing comfort to others in similarly bleak situations. By sharing their

sufferings, they arrive at a place of comfort. Because of the incomprehensible nature of this interaction between comfort and suffering, I know it is the work of God.

THE COMMUNITY OF SUFFERING

One of the reasons I am so passionate about helping people come to grips with their excessities, *Gotta Have It!* behaviors, is because of the suffering that lies at the heart. In my personal and professional life, I have never seen an excessity provide lasting relief in the long run. On the contrary, the excessity not only masks the suffering and thus the true need for comfort, but also often contributes to even more suffering.

CHRIS'S STORY

Chris felt battered and bruised by life. When he got into his car, it seemed like all the other drivers were idiots; driving to work was a real chore. Arriving at work didn't really make him feel any better because, even though he never knew what the day would bring, he always felt underappreciated and overworked. It wasn't any better at home, where he felt vaguely disapproved of by his wife and consistently disrespected by his children. At forty-seven, he couldn't get up after sitting for any length of time without something somewhere hurting.

Drinking brought him a sense of relief. Alone in his study, a couple of drinks were just what he needed to take the edge off the day and build up a warm, hazy buffer against the problems that kept grim vigil in the hall. He knew they wouldn't go away, but for a time he didn't have to think about them. He didn't have to think about anything. Just drink his scotch, watch the television, and shut out the world.

Chris is like so many people who choose the temporary fix of their excessity over the deeper work of uncovering the source of suffering in their lives. Chris, like so many people, chose the death of a thousand cuts over emotional surgery to correct the true issue. They keep on believing their pain will go away if they continue to plaster it over with an excessity. The problem is that such a shortcut solution has no hope of lasting.

NOTHING GOLD CAN STAY

This life is based upon impermanence. Psalm 144:4 says, "Man is like a breath; his days are like a fleeting shadow." Anything that we create to be lasting is, because of our own fleeting nature, short lived at best.

I think one of the most poignant descriptions of the impermanence of life is the famous poem by Robert Frost called "Nothing Gold Can Stay." It is, appropriately, very brief and speaks about the fragile nature of nature itself, beginning with the golden miracle of a tiny leaf. Such a miracle, though, is temporary, with the inevitable withering of that golden leaf, and leaf by leaf after that. The poem ends by lamenting,

So dawn goes down to day. / Nothing gold can stay.[1]

We hold on to our excessities like they are golden leaves, but they were never meant to stay. Any comfort they produce cannot last.

Planting Seeds

For a chapter on comfort, I have no doubt most of you found parts of it uncomfortable. For that, I offer no apologies because my desire is for you to come to grips with your false comforts and to rekindle your search for true comfort. In this Planting Seeds section, I'm going to ask you to do both.

In the last chapter, you examined and identified your excessities. In this section, you will look at each of them in light of how they play into your feelings of comfort and discomfort. In order to do that, I'm not going to go down a list of specific behaviors. (Remember, one person's comfort is another person's discomfort in the same situation.) Instead, I want you to use your list of excessities that are specific to you.

After you've done that, I'd like to go at this from a bit of a different direction. Thinking about discomfort, I'd like you to write down all of the things that cause you discomfort. These could be situations, feelings, or people. I'd like you to use the beginning phrase "I don't like it when …"

You might put down, "I don't like it when other people don't listen to me" or "I don't like it when I have to talk to people I don't know" or "I don't like it when I don't have enough money to pay my bills" or "I don't like it when I feel unattractive" or "I don't like it when I have to worry about my kids." Again, there will be as many unique "I don't like it when …" statements as there are people reading this book. Just keep going with this "I don't like it when …" exercise until you can't come up with anything else.

If you have trouble, pretend you're talking to a good friend—you know, the one you always call or talk to when you want to complain about your day. Think of it as a rant-and-rave session on paper. Everyone should be able to come up with at least one!

I don't like it when …

Each of the situations you described above causes you some level of discomfort. Within each situation, you get discouraged, angry, frustrated, upset, scared—something that falls under the heading of distress and unease. When you experience discomfort, you probably reach for something that will provide you relief from the discomfort and provide you with comfort.

I'd like you to look at each of your "I don't like it when …" statements and compare those to your list of excessities from the previous chapter. Be honest and write down if you find yourself engaging in one of your *Gotta Have It!* behaviors when confronted with an "I don't like it when …" situation. Whenever you do this, you are using an excessity to provide comfort, to make the bad feelings of your "I don't like it when …" go away.

For those of you who pride yourself in getting the test done quickly and are confident you've gotten all the answers right, I'm going to ask you to do this twice. The second time, s-l-o-w d-o-w-n, and really work through what you've written. Don't just assume that because you come up with an answer quickly it's the only answer there is or even the right answer. You are dealing with the human capacity for denial and misdirection. Factor that in, and give yourself time and breathing space to work through this exercise, recognizing that insight, not speed, is the goal.

Lastly, I'd like you to meditate on what your true needs for comfort are. Put another way, what are the real reasons behind your discomfort, your suffering? Earlier, we looked at Scripture and found the following reasons for needing comfort. Do you resonate with any of these?

Because of a hard life of work and toil—do you feel ground down by life and how hard it is?

Because of the death of a loved one—have you experienced the physical death of someone close, the death of a relationship, or even the death of a dream in your life?

Because of prejudice and oppression—are you the recipient of hostility and harm, or are others taking advantage of you?

Because of physical illness—are you experiencing an unexpected affliction, a chronic physical condition, or even a spiritual wasting away?

Because of catastrophic life circumstances—do you fear you are or are about to become overwhelmed by life and what it brings?

Because of a broken heart—do you feel yourself shattered by circumstance and wonder how you'll find the strength to heal and move forward?

Because of suffering—do you feel you're living in your own private hell because of the pain in your life?

When you can identify the source of your true need for comfort, unencumbered by the camouflage of your excessities, you can put your energies into addressing them—and then your excessities will naturally loosen their grip on your life.

The good news in all of this is that God is ready, willing, and able to comfort you in whatever suffering you experience. In the midst of all of suffering, the psalmist was able to say this to God: "Remember your word to your servant, for you have given me hope. My comfort in my suffering is this: Your promise preserves my life" (Ps. 119:49–50).

Today, God's Word is also for you, and it is His desire to give you hope, to give you comfort in the midst of suffering, for God has promised to walk that particular road with you.

In the midst of my pain, God, I cry out
to You, the source of hope and comfort.
I confess I have reached for too many

other things in order to be comforted. I have made those other things my god and set them up as idols in my life. I worshipped at those altars every time I turned to them and not to You to provide me with comfort. Help me find balance in my life. Help me find more of You in my life.

4

Our Need for Reassurance

Do not be anxious about anything,
but in everything, by prayer and
petition, with thanksgiving, present
your requests to God. (Phil. 4:6)

We live in an anxious world, and one of our deepest needs is to be reassured in the midst of our anxiety. Paul, in Philippians, tells us we should quell our anxiety through prayer and petition. Instead, however, we have reached for everything from pills to pasta, working to workouts, pull tabs to Prozac—without any lasting reassurance.

In our anxious world, we cry out, "It's not going to be okay!" as we come face-to-face with our fears, worries, and anxieties. In this world, we can feel vulnerable or at risk, often without being able to clearly identify why. We feel in danger, and the higher the sense of danger, the greater the need for reassurance. Often, reassurance comes through an excessity. In this chapter, I want you to examine if fear, worry, or anxiety is at the root of any of your *Gotta Have It!* behaviors.

CARLA'S STORY

Carla could feel that tinge of panic starting. Because of an amazingly busy week, complicated by a persistent head cold, she had gone three days without exercising. She was starting to feel jumpy, irritable, like she wanted to crawl out of her own skin. She needed to exercise; things weren't right in her world if she didn't. Exercise kept the monsters at bay. Carla had lived intimately connected to the monsters of low self-esteem, poor body image, and fear of fat for years. She relied on the feeling of pushing herself to the limit, giving herself an edge over those insecurities.

Exercising, for Carla, had become exorcising; when she exercised physically, she emotionally exorcised her monsters, her anxieties. Nothing else she did kept the panic under control. If she could just get back to exercising, everything would be fine—or at least back at status quo. She never felt she was really accomplishing anything by exercising, but at least she wasn't losing ground to the monsters. After three days, she could feel that ground start to shift.

For Carla, exercise was an excessity, truly a *Gotta Have It!* activity. Exercise soothed her worry and panic. After she exercised, she felt reassured that the disaster she lived with every day, lurking on the sidelines, would not happen—at least not today. Carla lived in fear of becoming fat. At the root of this fear was a tremendous insecurity about who she was as a person. Carla worked very hard to keep her outside "perfect" because she felt so imperfect on the inside. If she ever became fat, then the worst would happen—her outside would mirror her inside, and she would no longer be able to hide. Carla lived in fear of exposure. Being thin was her defensive barrier, and she was willing to do just about anything to shore up that defense.

Some of you can immediately identify with Carla. For the rest of you, however, before you automatically say, "Whew! That isn't *me*," I want you to take a moment to reconsider. Sometimes your *Gotta Have It!* behavior isn't meant to usher in things that make you feel good, but rather that behavior is meant to keep out things that make you feel bad. Fear, worry, and anxiety can make you feel bad—and they can become all-consuming, fueling those particular excessities tied to them. If you want to defuse the power of your excessities, you need to determine what negative feelings are at the heart of any of them.

GENERALIZED ANXIETY DISORDER

Many of the people I work with are burdened by fear, worry, and anxiety affecting their ability to live productive and happy lives. These same feelings propel them headlong into excessities. Often, they are focused on the negativity associated with their excessities, such as obesity or alcoholism or addiction to pornography. They want help to "just stop" whatever those things are that have taken control over their lives, as if those things were merely actions. It is a deeper issue, however, to work through their fear at the heart of those actions. Often, the source has been blown completely out of proportion. They are consumed with the what-ifs and what-abouts instead of recognizing the what-is.

According to the National Institute of Mental Health, almost seven million adults will experience a condition known as generalized anxiety disorder (GAD) in any given year.[1] GAD is a chronic condition where a person lives with anxiety, worry, and tension, even when there is little outside reason for it. This fear is accompanied by a variety of physical symptoms, such as fatigue, headaches, muscle tension, muscle-aches, difficulty swallowing, trembling, twitching, irritability, sweating, and hot flashes.[2] It's as if you're all ready for the fight of your life but can't really see who your enemy is. The true enemy is fear.

Generalized anxiety disorder falls under the category of anxiety disorders, which also includes panic disorder, obsessive-compulsive disorder, post-traumatic stress disorder, social phobia, and other phobias (such as agoraphobia).

As you read through explanations of each of these conditions, I'd like you to examine whether or not it is possible one or more of them are fueling some of your excessities. You don't need to be officially diagnosed as having one of these disorders to be able to recognize whether or not something about it resonates with you. Carla wasn't ever diagnosed as obsessive-compulsive, yet her extreme need to exercise contains some OCD components. Keep that in mind as you read these explanations from the National Institute of Mental Health.

> ***Panic Disorder***—this debilitating condition is when a person is seized suddenly by intense feelings of terror, fear, and impending loss of control. It is accompanied by a racing heart, feeling sweaty, weak, faint, or dizzy, and is often interpreted by the person as a heart attack.[3]

> ***Obsessive-Compulsive Disorder***—this is a condition where a person is plagued by

incessant, unwanted thoughts (obsessions) and/or repetitive behaviors (compulsions).[4] The person often develops the repetitive behaviors as a way to guard against or mitigate the unwanted thoughts. The repetitive behaviors can include things like hand washing, counting, cleaning, or checking things. The person hopes doing these rituals will prevent or guard against the obsessive thoughts. While doing the rituals provides temporary relief, not doing the rituals actually adds to the person's anxiety.

Post-Traumatic Stress Disorder—this reaction is the result of a terrifying event or situation where the person experienced or expected to receive serious injury. The clarity of the danger is so real, so immediate, it continues to intrude into the person's life—producing feelings of stress and panic—even when there is no longer any danger.[5] It's as if, once activated, their fight-or-flight response refuses to shut off, leaving them feeling numb and detached from life and those they love. They may also experience trouble sleeping.

Social Phobia—a person with a social phobia views social situations as battlefields, places of extreme danger. It affects fifteen million adult Americans in any given year.[6] In social situations, they are terrified of being watched and judged by other people, sure they will in some way be humiliated or embarrassed. Eating around or speaking to other people is sheer torture.[7]

Phobias—social phobias can lead to other phobias, such as agoraphobia. People with panic disorders can also develop agoraphobia, as they seek to avoid any situation or place that produced a panic attack in the past. Their list of "safe places" becomes smaller and smaller.

All of these conditions have at their base fear, worry, and anxiety. These can be hard taskmasters when acceded to and given control over your life. When those negative feelings take on larger-than-life proportions, they produce feelings of panic and dread even on a day when the sky is blue, the air is clean, and the sun is shining. The more feelings of panic they produce, the more apt you are to seek out behaviors that produce reassurance that all is well—or, at least, all is well for right now. Excessities can become a close-your-eyes, plug-your-ears, sing-la-la-la-la-la activity to drown out the drumbeat of fear, worry, and anxiety.

WHAT AND WHY TO FEAR

Fear is a God-given emotional response. He meant for us to use it, yet He didn't mean for us to be paralyzed by it. Somehow, fear has gotten loose from the purpose God intended. And too many times, we're the ones who have opened the gate.

Fear is not necessarily always a bad thing. In fact, reasonable fear is a great motivator. It can help move you to prepare for a significant situation, such as a natural disaster. Fear can keep you from walking on railroad tracks or crossing a busy street or working on your toaster while it's still plugged in. This is fear based upon collective wisdom or personal experience.

Unreasonable fear is fear that is outside its boundaries. This is fear that has no relation to reality. Unreasonable fear says because it has happened before, it must always happen, and there is no margin of error. Unreasonable fear says that "might" or "could" must be interpreted as "will" and "should." Unreasonable fear demands a preeminent place in our lives, dictating what we will do, where we will go, how we will feel, what we will forfeit, and what we will value. Unreasonable fear is our creation and is not the kind of fear that God wants us to have.

It is appropriate to fear that which has power over you. The challenge comes in knowing exactly what that is. People with social phobias believe other people have the power to embarrass and humiliate them, so they fear social situations. In truth, the only power of that kind is the power you give someone. Open the gate of fear to other people, and you will find yourself corralled. People with obsessive-compulsive disorder believe their rituals hold the key to controlling fear. In truth, their rituals control them by keeping them chained to their fear. People with generalized anxiety disorder live daily keeping their eyes to the ground, watching for any sign of something to fear, often oblivious to the true storm clouds forming in the sky above. This produces a life spent fearing the wrong things and suffering for it—as well as missing the right things and suffering for that, too.

WORRY

Trina was a worrier. She'd been one as long as she could remember. She worried about how she looked and what others thought of her. She worried about what she wore and what she ate. She worried about her schoolwork and her grades. She'd wake up in the morning and begin to go down her list of worries, checking off the steps she'd taken to avoid them. She worried about things that happened, and she worried about things that didn't.

As an adult, her worrying continued unabated. She worried about her job and how her supervisors perceived her. She still worried about her looks and what others thought of her. She worried about her relationships but got married anyway. Once married, she took up worrying about her husband, as well as herself. When she had children, her sphere of worry quickly ballooned to encompass every conceivable problem, danger, trouble, or disaster that could possibly happen to her children as well. All of this worrying left her tired, grouchy, unappreciated, tense, and stretched thin. She had long since gotten over any joy in being able to say, "I told you so," when her worried predictions actually came to pass. It didn't matter so much that they did; what mattered more to Trina was that they *could*.

For some people, worry itself can almost be classified as an excessity—as a *Gotta Have It!* behavior—because of how quickly they default to a worry position. For them, a state of worry is a state of familiarity. Perhaps for you, worry allows you to prepare for any possible eventuality—and because there's no real need to prepare for something positive, the eventualities you prepare for always range from bad to worse. Because you are so familiar with and so good at the worry game, your range is broad and all encompassing: A negative comment from your boss today means you're going to be fired tomorrow. A stomachache today means an ulcer tomorrow. A headache is a brain aneurysm. A gained pound is obesity. And on and on it goes. When anything's possible, there's no limit to the possible calamity. In some ways, worry is like watching a movie—except it's your own private disaster film. That internal viewing can be so compelling, you're blinded to reality. The *what-ifs* crowd out the *what-is*. Worry is a real scene-stealer, and the scenes being stolen are bits of your life.

When worry is your default setting, you will often turn to excessities in order to provide just a little white noise to drown out worry's drumbeat. Often, the excessity is food. I have known people who could eat to their feelings of worry the same as someone mindlessly munches popcorn at the movie theater or a bag of chips while watching television. Eating and worry can go hand in hand, like drinking coffee and smoking a cigarette.

Worry, with its constant "on" switch, negatively impacts health. Every week, it seems, we are inundated by another study showing the deleterious effects of worry and stress on our lives. Generally, these are followed up by advertisements touting the latest thing to magically ease our worries and make all that stress melt away. But if any of these things actually worked in the long term, our collective worry would be decreasing, not increasing, along with our need for the latest deworrier.

One of the reasons Jesus came to earth was to help explain to us the way things really are. Remember what Jesus said about worry:

> Therefore I tell you, do not worry about your life, what you will eat or drink; or about your body, what you will wear. Is not life more important than food, and the body more important than clothes? Look at the birds of the air; they do not sow or reap or stow away in barns, and yet your heavenly Father feeds them. Are you not much more valuable than they? Who of you by worrying can add a single hour to his life?

> And why do you worry about clothes? See how the lilies of the field grow. They do not labor or spin. Yet I tell you that not even Solomon in all his splendor was dressed like one of these. If that is how God clothes the grass of the field, which is here today and tomorrow is thrown into the fire, will he not much more clothe you, O you of little faith? So do not worry, saying, "What

shall we eat" or "What shall we drink?" or "What shall we wear?" For the pagans run after all these things, and your heavenly Father knows that you need them. But seek first his kingdom and his righteousness, and all these things will be given to you as well. Therefore do not worry about tomorrow, for tomorrow will worry about itself. Each day has enough trouble of its own. (Matt. 6:25–34)

Every time I read this passage, I am struck by the types of things Jesus says not to worry about. He says not to worry about what you'll eat, what you'll drink, or what you'll wear. As you read earlier, these are definite needs; they are even identified as such. Yet Jesus says you're not to worry about them. That would seem like a flippant, "just don't" kind of response to a very real concern if it weren't for the reason Jesus gives. He says you're not to worry about them because God already knows you need them.

Worry, it appears, takes far too much time and energy away from more important things, like seeking God's kingdom and His righteousness. Worry is nonproductive. In the Planting Seeds section I'm going to ask you to write down all of the things you worry about. I, like you, must confess that my list will be far too long. That is the nature of worry.

Worry is like an illustration I remember seeing of the levee system in New Orleans during Hurricane Katrina. On the top of the water, the concrete walls of the levee looked so massive and strong.

However, under the water the relentless wave action of the water was gradually eating away at the earthen berm upon which the concrete wall stood. Wave by wave, a little more of the earth was gouged out and exposed to the corrosive power of the water. Eventually, the foundation upon which the levee wall stood was completely undermined—and it failed, allowing the water to rush in and flood the area.

I think worry is like that. Wave by wave, gradually over time, worry eats away at the foundations of our lives, at our emotional, relational, physical, and spiritual foundations. Jesus says the answer to worry is to choose not to and instead put your efforts and time into concentrating on the things of God. This activity, by its very nature, will shore up and strengthen your foundations.

ANXIETY

Anxiety is fear, worry, and apprehension all rolled into one. It is an overwhelming belief that the worst is coming and that you absolutely are not prepared to handle it. Anxiety produces panic and dread. The feelings of doom and disaster are so real, it can prompt you to run toward destructive behaviors as the lesser of two evils. In this case, the excessity functions not so much to produce pleasure as to throw up a buffer against those feelings of anxiety. As such, the excessity is given carte blanche; it is ceded a great deal of latitude and power because of the desperation and fear of the anxiety.

When you experience anxiety, God does not want you running to an excessity; He wants you running to Him. The verse that started this chapter says that you and I are not to be anxious about anything but that in everything, by prayer and petition, we are to tell God what we need to deal with our anxiety. This verse is amazing in its all-encompassing nature with its use of the words *anything* and *everything*.

God knows that only He is able to counter the power that anxiety can exert over our lives. If you are anxious, you are to give it over to God completely, totally, without reserve. You are also to adjust your thinking from being anxious to being grateful, which is quite a shift! Being grateful, however, is a very useful tool because it forces you to concentrate on the good things instead of the bad. Anxiety scoops up any possible bad thing, with the cyclonic power of an emotional whirlwind, and sends you spinning wildly out of control. Gratitude, however, is an anchor, tethering you to God through a remembrance and acknowledgment of the good things. Gratitude also redirects your thinking away from all the things you can't control, toward all of the things God can.

Anxiety, in my experience, is like a runaway train. The longer it goes on uncontrolled, the more speed it picks up … until it is screaming down the track of your thoughts, pushing anything and everything else out of its way. Only God, through the divine communion found in prayer, through His Spirit, is able to slow that train down and put your thoughts back on a proper track. Prayer allows your mind to rest, to surrender over to God instead of surrendering to the panic. When you do this, God promises that He will give you His peace. Peace and panic cannot exist in the same space. They are mutually exclusive. Peace is the true antidote for anxiety, not a cover-it-over, just-make-it-all-go-away *Gotta Have It!* excessity.

Planting Seeds

Fear is very powerful, so before we delve into this section, I want you to be honest about whether or not you're ready to dig deeper into this area of your own fears, worries, and anxieties. Even thinking about doing so may cause one or more of your excessities to begin to tug at your attention. Excessities are classic diversions where fears, worries, and anxieties are concerned. (If you feel one or more of them tugging at you right now, write them down! They have just revealed themselves to you!)

If this is very uncomfortable, I encourage you to do some of the following to prepare:

Pray for God to cover you with His peace as you go through this.

Find a comfortable, safe place.

If you need to, get into a favorite set of clothes.

Wrap yourself in a comfortable blanket.

Brew yourself a cup of hot tea.

Set out a picture of loved ones to remind you that working toward wholeness and healing is a valuable activity and not for yourself alone.

Arrange to have a family member or trusted friend with you as you do this activity.

Give yourself permission to set aside a different time to do this activity. Be sure to specify a day, time, and place.

If you are somewhat uncomfortable, let me just say that is perfectly understandable. Fears, worries, and anxieties are not easy things to consider. Most people go to great lengths to avoid dealing with them. This is part of the denial and avoidance system we set up. I will ask you to go ahead and continue anyway, working through as much as you're able. It is fine to take a break, put the book down, take a walk, say a prayer, call a friend.

Because so much of our *Gotta Have It!* activities are a distraction, I'd like you to take some time and put a name to your fears. I'd like you to answer the question, "What am I afraid of?" Again, don't just stop at the first destination and consider the journey done. Follow the trail. Examine each fear, and try to follow it back to its inception. You may say to yourself that you are afraid of other people, but what is it about other people that you are afraid of? Are you afraid of the way they make you feel? Are you afraid of what they will think of you? Are you afraid of being hurt by them? Are you afraid of being vulnerable to others? When have you felt vulnerable and in danger? This is the sort of working back I'd like you to do.

Go ahead and begin the journey:

What am I afraid of?

Next, I'd like you to think about all the things you worry about. Include the things you worry about for yourself, your family, your friends, and your acquaintances—even what you worry about for where you live or for the country. Worries can often seem less bothersome than fears, but what they lack in intensity they often make up in sheer volume! Go ahead and write down:

What do I worry about?

Next, go back over your fears and worries, and mark any that cause you anxiety. These will be the ones that cause your heart rate to quicken and your muscles to tense. These will become special items of prayer for you in the coming weeks and months, as I'd like you to commit to praying about these whenever you feel anxious about them.

My Special Prayer List:

1.

2.

3.

4.

5.

Now that you've become more acquainted with your fears, worries, and anxieties, I'd like you to examine your excessities and determine which ones you use to cope. These will be behaviors you want to watch for as they may signal you are feeling fearful, worried, or anxious before you even consciously become aware of it.

When that happens, stop what you're doing, and meditate on why you feel compelled to engage in that activity. Ask yourself these questions:

Where am I?

How am I feeling?

Is there something that triggered feeling this way?

Can I identify any specific fear, worry, or anxiety I'm feeling?

By taking this break, am I able to feel better?

After taking this break, do I still want to engage in my behavior?

Is there something else I can do to make myself feel better that would be better for me?

Most people are conditioned to run from their fears. I
would like you to try instead to face them and become very well
acquainted with them. The only way I know to do this is through
the shield of faith and by the power of prayer. Ask God to stand
as your defender against your fears. Commit to placing any
fear you have as subordinate to your fear of God, and give Him
dominion over your fears. Call upon His name and His power to
protect you.

King David spent a great deal of his time afraid, under attack,
besieged by people and events. He countered these times of
fear, worry, and anxiety by calling up images of God, by praying
to God, and by being thankful. The psalms of David are an excel-
lent place to find these visual images and prayers that you can
use when confronting your own fears. Below are just a few of the
ways David and the other psalmists saw God:

As a Shield (Ps. 3:3)

As a Refuge (Ps. 9:9)

As a Rock (Ps. 18:2)

As a Shepherd (Ps. 23:1)

As a Savior (Ps. 25:5)

As a Stronghold (Ps. 27:1)

As a Fortress (Ps. 31:3)

As a Deliverer (Ps. 40:17)

As a Light (Ps. 43:3)

As a Father (Ps. 68:5)

Lord, there are many things I am afraid of! Help me conquer my fears, my worries, and my anxieties and give each and every one of them over to You. I claim the images of David and ask You to fill my mind with these images of You to banish my fears. I pray the promise of Isaiah 33:6, that You will be my sure foundation, one that does not give way to fear, worry, or anxiety. I pray that You will be my rich store of salvation, wisdom, and knowledge. I claim the fear of You, Lord, as the key to this treasure.

5

Our Need for Security

Woe to those who go down to Egypt for help,
who rely on horses, who trust in the multitude of
their chariots and in the great strength of their
horsemen, but do not look to the Holy One of
Israel, or seek help from the LORD. (Isa. 31:1)

I haven't put in a call to Egypt lately or enlarged my garage to fit a chariot, but I can still relate to this Isaiah verse. In the search for security, all of us run toward our perceived protection. The less secure we feel, the faster we run and the tighter we cling. Like a two-year-old with a blankie, letting go just doesn't seem to be an option.

CRAIG'S STORY

Craig didn't like getting older. It messed with the mental picture he had of himself as perpetually in his early twenties. That was when he felt the most vital, the most alive, the most in control of his world. He could hit a drive like Phil and a jump shot like Kobe. He'd been single in his early twenties, without family obligations and responsibilities like he had now. Craig wanted to stay suspended in that moment in time, even though the earth kept revolving underneath him and time marched on.

He joined a variety of gyms over the years and used all of them to tell himself he'd get fit soon. He kept buying costly golf clubs, sure that the next expensive innovation with the titanium shaft and computer-designed "sweet spot" was just the one to do the trick and give him back his edge. Craig bought a low-slung, high-octane sports car that he took out of the garage whenever the sun was out and his wife was gone. Always on the lookout for the next big financial deal, he lost track of the money he'd "invested" over the years, so sure the next one would prove once and for all his business acumen. Whenever he had the opportunity and—according to his wife— sometimes when he didn't, he chose to dress like someone fifteen years younger. He knew the places to shop where the latest urban styles were "upsized" to fit more mature physiques.

His friends were of two different sets: a younger group of men, generally golfing or basketball buddies, who made him feel as though he had shed years if not pounds—and an older set, generally business acquaintances, whose greater age always cemented his status as Craig the Younger. Craig had few friends or even significant acquaintances his own age. He didn't really feel comfortable with men his own age. Instead, he liked younger men because that's how he saw himself, and older men because they always seemed to have something to offer.

Craig made sure he had all the latest gadgets so popular with the younger set. If he heard about something one week, he made sure to buy it the next. This caused his wife to roll her eyes and bemoan one more "whatever," but Craig figured that it was his money and that he had a right to spend it on whatever he wanted. What he really wanted was to be considered relevant and young. If spending a few hundred dollars, or often more, could achieve that feeling, well, it was a bargain. The younger guys were jealous of what he could buy because they knew what it was, and the older guys were impressed because they didn't. Either way, it put Craig in the driver's seat, just like he was twentysomething all over again.

SECURITY BLANKET

Tied to the need for reassurance that we examined in the previous chapter is a deep need for security—or, rather, for *feeling secure*. As toddlers, this need often manifests itself as attraction to some sort of physical object, like a security blanket, that calms fears and helps provide a feeling of well-being. I've also seen this security blanket be a favorite stuffed animal or toy or a scuffed-up pair of too-tight shoes or a well-worn shirt. It's hard to know what children will pick, but something about their "whatever" makes them feel safe and protected.

Perhaps this blanket or toy or pair of shoes or shirt is our first *Gotta Have It!* object. It is where we test how it feels to demand and be satisfied. We say quite loudly *Gotta Have It!* about this item and generally get our way, at least for a while. It is where we first use an outside thing to make our insides feel better.

Lisa was unable to sleep as an adult if she could not smell laundry detergent on her bed linens. The world was not a safe place to her without that olfactory security blanket. Quite naturally, this required her to launder her sheets multiple times per week. This particular security blanket was fairly easy to work around, as long as she had enough detergent at home. Others have been much more disruptive.

Claire couldn't go more than two or three days without shopping for clothes. She loved the promise of a new outfit. Having something new in her closet or drawer meant safety. It also meant spending thousands of dollars every year and having closets and drawers full of nearly new clothes. When things got too crowded, she'd bundle them up, stuff them into a bag, and put them out on the curb for the thrift-store truck, which collected from her every three months like clockwork.

All of these things are really grown-up pacifiers, established calming behaviors to provide a sense of security in the midst of an unsettling world. We've already looked at how often these pacifiers are food based. Have a tough day—reach for a donut or a bowl of ice cream. Get into a fight with your spouse—grab the bag of chips and bean dip. Feel anxious or nervous—burrow into the safety of a box of cookies or bag of M&M's.

These strategies are meant to make us feel more secure. They are the handholds we reach for when our lives get rocky and our emotions unstable. You may look at some of the examples I've given and think they're pretty frivolous, like laundry soap, which seems like a small thing. But no matter how small the blanket, the safety it represents is huge.

Whether your security blanket is big or small, I'd like you to think about where you go and what you do when you feel insecure. I'd like you to think about why those things help you feel secure. These security blankets are what you have come to trust to make you feel better. As a toddler, you may have had an actual blanket.

As an adult, that security blanket may come wrapped as an excessity. To help you with this, I've highlighted a few of the more significant handholds I've seen used over the years as grown-up, adult security blankets.

MONEY

"In God We Trust" has been engraved on our coins since 1864. Somewhere in the intervening years, however, it seems we've shifted from trust in God to trust in the coin itself. This isn't a recent phenomenon; it's been happening for a long time. King Solomon, in his book of wisdom known as Proverbs, puts it this way: "The wealth of the rich is their fortified city; they imagine it an unscalable wall" (Prov. 18:11).

There are many people today for whom wealth is their unscalable wall. They truly believe if they acquire enough of it, build up a high enough wall of it, the cares and concerns of the world will not be able to climb over. The problem, of course, lies in the fact that cares and concerns have very creative ways of mounting siege ramps against the walls of wealth and breach even the highest parapets. Insecurities also find ways to tunnel under the strongest edifices.

Money, quite simply, is not a secure enough thing to put your trust in. Again, from Proverbs: "Do not wear yourself out to get rich; have the wisdom to show restraint. Cast but a glance at riches, and they are gone, for they will surely sprout wings and fly off to the sky like an eagle" (23:4–5). Money is a fluid, dynamic entity, and its worth is based upon factors out of the control of most people. A person's wealth can be made and lost within a single year. How many people have won millions of dollars on a lottery one year, only to wind up losing it all within a short span of time? How many people put their trust in the wealth they committed to Bernie Madoff, only to lose every cent in his billion-dollar Ponzi scheme? Money is not an appropriate place to look for security.

Money can be made and even more money made … and still not be enough, as we saw previously when we looked at money. This is especially true if money and acquiring money have become an excessity. Revisit the Solomon quote in Ecclesiastes: "Whoever loves money, never has money enough; whoever loves wealth is never satisfied with his income. This too is meaningless" (Eccl. 5:10). Solomon was the wealthiest person of his day, above all the other kings on earth. He was incredibly wealthy and incredibly wise. He knew that wealth and acquiring wealth can become a black-hole, *Gotta Have It!* excessity. Perceiving money as security can create an obsession with money and the things money can buy. And because money can, quite frankly, buy a great deal, there is a tendency to assign it more power than it is due; there is a tendency to trust it more than is wise.

Money is not permanent because it can be lost in the blink of an eye (or in the crash of the stock market, or in the devaluation of currency, or through theft or malfeasance or cooked books). It is not permanent in the here and now, and it's absolutely irrelevant in the hereafter. Money may get you some traction when you're alive, but it is useless to you when you're dead: "Do not be overawed when a man grows rich, when the splendor of his house increases; for he will take nothing with him when he dies, his splendor will not descend with him" (Ps. 49:16–17). In cruder, present-day language: The hearse doesn't come with a trailer.

Money promises to provide security, but it often creates the opposite: "A man's riches may ransom his life, but a poor man hears no threat" (Prov. 13:8). The more stock you set in the things you have, including money and the things money can buy, the greater the threat of losing it all. Those who have much have much to lose. Those with little, sleep under a lesser threat of loss and can feel more secure.

Money can be a source of security, but it can also be a source of heartburn: "The sleep of a laborer is sweet, whether he eats little or much, but the abundance of a rich man permits him no sleep" (Eccl. 5:12). If you put all your security eggs in the money basket, then you must perpetually worry about eggs breaking and losing both.

POWER

Money is often the outward venue for a different kind of security blanket—the covering of power. Power is a heady tonic for insecurity. It provides a sense of invincibility and the illusion of control. Power, like money, is notoriously shifty. Solomon puts it this way: "For riches do not endure forever, and a crown is not secure for all generations" (Prov. 27:24). Money and power are transitory.

Money and power can certainly be linked, but the pursuit of power does not always involve money. Some people look to power as a way to protect themselves from a dangerous and hurtful world—for control over the situations they find themselves in and for control over the people they are surrounded by.

Because it is treacherously difficult to have power over situations, this need for power is often transferred to more controllable commodities. This power grab is a need to exert power and control over people. If the people around you can be made to do what you want, when you want, in the way you want, the world is more secure. There are fewer surprises.

This is a strategy with a very short shelf life because people generally do not like being controlled. Either they will actively rebel against it, or they will passively work around it. Either way, there inevitably will come a day when that power ceases to be effective. The person discovers he no longer has the power in the relationship, and he quite often no longer has the relationship.

Even if power is effective for a longer period of time, it has an end date: "What man can live and not see death, or save himself from the power of the grave?" (Ps. 89:48). That end date is the second one on your headstone. Earthly power is tethered to the temporary. It may seem like a surefire bet in this life, but all bets are off in the next. Power has a short-term effect and is not secure. Using it to procure security is, as Solomon said, "meaningless."

FAME, STATUS, SUCCESS—REAL OR IMAGINED

There is a corollary to money and power that I have seen people cling to as a way to security. It is the desire for fame, status, or success as a bulwark against feelings of marginalization and lack of self-esteem. These people often feel that they are outside the rules that control the rest of society.

Special status bestowed by others is precarious because it is usually based upon the current popular culture. Popular culture is not stable. There was a time when politicians had status; now they are thought of more as infamous than famous. There was a time when the bankers on Wall Street with million-dollar bonuses were looked upon with something akin to reverence; now it's more like revulsion. The special people in a society can change overnight. When the winds shift and you're not considered special anymore, your world can come crashing down. Just ask past-their-prime athletes, last year's beautiful people, or former child-star actors relegated to third-rate reality shows.

I have known a few people who were famous because of their achievements or position. I have known far more people who assigned themselves their own special status. Often they considered themselves to be special and outside of the rules, not so much because of what they had but because of what they *didn't* have. This is not popularity through the positive but notoriety through the negative. Their special status was because "no one else has suffered like I have" or "I am owed because of what I've lacked in my life" or "because of what I've suffered I can't be held responsible." This attitude produces a sense of entitlement. Yet this sense of entitlement isn't bestowed upon the person by popular consensus. Rather, it is *that person* who has elevated himself or herself to a special status.

When you have declared yourself special and demand special treatment because of it, you create a false sense of security. After all, you are in control because you have declared yourself the sole arbiter of your specialness. The instability of this platform arises because others may not be of the same opinion. They may interpret your specialness as rude, aggressive, argumentative, insensitive, arrogant, or unrealistic. The more you loudly demand your specialness, the deeper their negative reaction is driven. The more you demand to live outside the rules, the more others may desire for you to simply live outside of their proximity.

It is seductive to want to live outside of the rules and the natural consequences of life. Rules so often have to do with limits and restrictions. Natural consequences can seem harsh and unfair. The *Gotta Have It!* of claiming a special status yells out, "That doesn't apply to me!" When we get to avoid the rules of others and make up our own rules, we feel a sense of control over our world. When we are in control, we feel more secure.

PHYSICAL APPEARANCE

Relying on your looks, on your physical attractiveness, is a strategy. It is a strategy deployed to produce advantage. This is a true excessity. Because of the very transient nature of physical attractiveness, it can diminish over time and through circumstance. This is because physical attractiveness, while a universal concept, has an individual component to it. That which is attractive today may not be so tomorrow and that which is attractive to one may not be so to another. Looks and physical attractiveness are notoriously shifting sands, even in the best of times.

Getting by on your looks, however, is a timeworn strategy. It usually starts in childhood when you begin to perceive that people, generally adults, will make exceptions for you because of the way you look. You discover that you are "cute" and that this is advantageous. As you mature, you begin to realize this "cuteness" can morph into something more powerful—physical attractiveness—especially to members of the opposite sex. Left unchecked, this reliance on physical attributes to provide security to your world can backfire into a variety of excessities, all designed to enhance and preserve physical appearance. This tendency is made even more desperate by the inescapable truth of age.

YOUTH AND AGE

We don't want to feel good about our aging; we want to reverse it. This is where the excessities of physical attractiveness merge into the excessities of antiaging, creating a resonance coupling of irrepressible forces. Because we are a society that venerates youth and not age, physical attractiveness is seen as the unique property of the young. If there is someone who is attractive later in life, the caveat is always that she looks great "for her age."

The quest for eternal youth has tremendous *Gotta Have It!* potential. If you doubt that, just watch Saturday afternoon or late-night television, and notice how many times you see something advertised as the next "gotta have" miracle to slow the progression of aging. From topical products to clothing, from nutritional supplements to surgical procedures, from exercise equipment to weight-loss formulas designed to melt off the fat *without* exercising, there is a new "gotta have" touted almost every commercial break.

Grabbing onto youth is a powerful *Gotta Have It!* behavior in order to feel secure. It transcends gender, sweeping up men and women alike. However, men tend to want to stay young in order to feel virile, whereas women tend to want to stay young in order to feel physically attractive. As a culture, we've gotten pretty creative coming up with ways to stay healthy longer and to mask our age. The reality, however, is that we age. Youth is a golden moment in time that does not last. Youthfulness is not a reliable, long-term strategy for security.

ANGER

We've talked about anger before, but I want to bring it up here because anger is a way many people deal with insecurity. Feeling insecure makes them feel vulnerable and places them in a defensive position. Often, in order to counteract this feeling of defenselessness, they will literally go on the offensive through anger. This can be the underground anger of passive-aggressiveness or the explosive anger of rage. When they feel insecure, they immediately vault ahead to full-blown anger, which catapults them out of that defensive and insecure position. Anger allows them to feel as if they have the upper hand, if not in circumstance, at least in their response to it. Anger makes them feel empowered, emboldened, and often invincible. Their security is not so much in mastering the situation as it is in mastering *caring* about the situation. Anger is a shield against feeling pain even if it is not effective in preventing the pain.

Anger, like everything else we've talked about here, cannot provide lasting security. It is, by its nature, driven by emotions. Emotions are infamously untrustworthy and changeable. Anger can take you to the heights of indignation and outrage one moment and plummet you to the depths of despair the next. Emotions are not a stable platform to anchor your security.

Planting Seeds

Even though security is notoriously difficult to find and maintain, it's still a basic need. Our trouble comes because we run to the wrong things in search of security and run away from the right things. Money, power, fame, status, success, looks, youthfulness, and anger are all things people often run toward in order to achieve security. They appear to be solid and able to provide the security we need. The key word here is "appear." As you and I know all too well, things are not always as they appear.

The question I'd like you to ask yourself for this chapter is *what do I look to in my life to provide security or to feel more secure?* What are your personal handholds when life gets rocky? They can be everything from a comforting smell to the amount in your bank account to the emotional satisfaction of an angry outburst.

Please realize that not everything on this list will be negative and that, hopefully, a great many of things you put down will be positive. The goal at this point is not to predetermine which is positive and which is negative but to put down every one you can think of. Think back over your past, to times when you felt especially insecure, and try to remember what it is you turned to during those times. View yourself where you are right now, and examine how you deal with insecurity in your life. Put yourself in the future, and think about anticipated storms. In the midst of the upheaval, what do you see yourself holding on to? Okay, now make your list:

What do I look to in my life to provide security or to feel
more secure?

1.

2.

3.

4.

5.

6.

7.

8.

9.

10.

Again, you may have more or less than ten. Don't become
focused on the number but on the truth. Really examine your
feelings, and leave yourself open to being uncomfortable as you
visualize yourself in situations of insecurity.

Beside each strategy, I'd like you put down the significant

times in your life when you found yourself using these handholds. What was happening in your life at that time? As much as possible, I'd like you to put down names, places, dates, events, details. These earthquake events are ones you want to be aware of, as they may be the source of aftershocks you feel in your life today.

Now, I'd like you to go over your list and divide it into two different categories. In one category put all of your strategies that actually produce a greater level of security. In the other category put all of your strategies that make you *feel* more secure. I think you will find that we have a great many more things that make us feel more secure than actually produce greater security.

Lastly, I'd like you to indicate whether—looking at it honestly right now—a particular strategy is really a positive or a negative in your life. I'm not asking if you think a particular strategy is effective. I have known many people who were highly effective using their anger as a way to counter insecurity. However, this strategy, though effective in the short run, was a significant negative to their health and their relationships. A strategy is positive if it builds you up, affirms your value and worth as an individual, and buffers you against the panic that insecurity can produce. A strategy is positive if it is effective without any negative side effects. These are the strategies you want to identify, maintain, and enhance.

As you identify negative strategies, these are the ones you want to work to eliminate from your security toolbox. They are broken, dangerous tools that need to be thrown away, no matter how long they've been in there or how attached you are to them. Build up your positives and boot out your negatives!

Before we leave this chapter and go on to the next, I'd like you to identify three meaningful ideas that have surfaced through this Planting Seeds exercise. I'd like you to mull over these three (or more, if you have them) and allow them to permeate your consciousness. They are the leaven of discovery.

My three meaningful ideas:

1.

2.

3.

Holy One of Israel, so many years ago You entreated the people to turn to You for safety and security instead of less reliable avenues. Help me learn by their example and not make the same mistakes over and over again. Help me turn to You for my safety and my security. In this world of uncertainty and broken promises, You alone are my Rock and my Refuge. I claim You as my strong tower and commit to turning to You when my world shakes. Keep me safe. Make me strong. Hold my hand.

6

Our Need for Validation

But I am a worm and not a man, scorned by men and despised by the people. All who see me mock me; they hurl insults, shaking their heads. (Ps. 22:6–7)

We long to be validated. If you grew up without validation, you look at the passage above and understand deep down those terrible words. You have felt like a worm, scorned and despised. You have been mocked, insulted, and dismissed in life. You have ached over the universal need to feel validated as a person. When others denied you this, you may have tried to validate yourself using external activities. When externals are used for self-validation, they often turn into ravenous excessities.

MEGAN'S STORY

Growing up, Megan was always trying to live up to the expectations of her parents. It wasn't that they were outwardly abusive; it was just that no matter what she did, she never quite measured up to their standards. Even if she came home with a good grade on a paper, project, or report card, there was always a little bit more she should have done.

When she went clothes shopping with her mother, Megan always felt diminished. She could remember putting on a new dress or shirt in the dressing room and feeling on top of the world until her mother looked her over. The reaction was always thoughtful and critical, as her mother tried to decide if her deficiencies were less than the cost of the garment. It was the same story when she got her hair cut. Her mother would stand next to the stylist, pointing out all of the problems, from frizzy, unruly hair to double cowlicks. Together, they would poke at her head and pull at her hair, frowning and discussing her shortcomings as if she wasn't sitting right there.

When they visited her grandparents or extended family, both of her parents were open and verbal about how well she was *almost* doing. It was as if they just couldn't say something nice—period—but had to throw in a distasteful tidbit that called any genuine praise into question. They talked about her behavior, her body, her schoolwork. When she got older, they threw in her friends, boyfriends, goals, and plans in life. At some point, Megan stopped sharing anything of significance with her parents altogether. Outwardly, she was compliant and obedient, divulging just enough details about her life to give them daily fodder for discussion without exposing herself to any meaningful scrutiny.

It was at this point Megan turned to other people for validation. Finding little—and none that was untainted—at home, her peers became paramount. There wasn't anything Megan wouldn't do to be "included" in middle school. She learned to alter her personality depending upon which group she was with, becoming a chameleon of sorts. Her true self she hid away, taking it out sporadically and only when she felt really safe with those one or two friends she could trust.

Her sophomore year in high school, Megan tried sex as a way to achieve validation. Once she got over the initial terror and humiliation of it, she began to realize she had the power to make herself valuable. In college, she invariably was drawn to partners who were analytical and critical like her parents. She kept hoping she could get one of them to love her unconditionally but found herself disappointed. Through numerous relationships and a failed marriage, she was still trying. And the more she tried, the worse she felt about herself.

SELF-WORTH

People who lack validation in their lives fail to understand their own value and worth. Without validation, it is difficult to have a concept of self-worth. Without an understanding of intrinsic value, a person will often look outside of self to find that validation. Instead of looking inside to anchor your belief in your value as a person, you hook that belief to the passing whims of circumstance, culture, and conditions. Your belief in your value as a person can be ripped from you, leaving you grasping for the next handhold to come along. This was Megan's life. Her hold on self-worth was only as strong as whatever relationship she was in. When that relationship ended, her sense of value as a person evaporated, leaving her frantic and desperate to begin another relationship. Within any relationship she had, she kept looking to the wrong party to anchor her sense of self.

She chose the person who always left instead of the person who was always there—Megan herself.

RANDY'S STORY

Randy grew up poor, with a chaotic family. His father drank too much and his mother ate too much. Both of them were so enmeshed in their own comfort behaviors they had very little time, energy, or money left for their four children, who tended to fend for themselves. Randy's older sister, Debbie, spent a good portion of her childhood taking care of the other kids, and she jettisoned Randy as soon as he got old enough to take care of himself.

He was ashamed of his family; ashamed of his father's drinking and general lack of ambition; ashamed of his mother's obesity and general lack of looks. It seemed like the components other families had to make them happy—a successful dad and a pretty mom—were denied him. Because he didn't have the right kind of family or very much money, Randy felt he had to work harder to be accepted in school by the more popular kids. He got a job as soon as he could so he could have money, and a new world opened up for him. The harder he worked, the more successful he was at his job. After he graduated from high school, Randy tried a few classes at community college but never really stuck with them because of his job, which was taking off. Before long, he was an assistant manager.

Randy felt like he had the power to reinvent himself as someone successful. This time, it didn't have anything to do with who his family was; he was in charge of his success. By the time he'd moved to a regional manager position halfway across the country, Randy thought he was fully in charge of his self-worth. The only problem was his self-doubt moved right along with him. Randy may have left his family behind, but the shame he felt stayed with him. Whenever that shame threatened to resurface, he pushed it down by weaving his sense of worth tighter into his successful career.

And then the economy tanked, and Randy began to seriously fear for his job. Twenty years out of high school and all of that insecurity came rushing back. If he lost his job, Randy felt he would lose himself. Without his job, he was nothing. Without his job, how could he hope to keep his family together? If he lost his job, his kids would look down on him like he'd looked down on his own father. If he lost his job, how long would it be before he lost his marriage? Randy was in a state of absolute panic. His anxiety was affecting his health, his family, and his job.

There is a reason why the term *self-worth* starts with the word *self.* It is not the worth of a person acknowledged and accepted by others; it is rather the worth of a person acknowledged and accepted by self. This self-worth is one of the key components in our ability to love ourselves. If we see ourselves as worthless, it's very difficult to generate self-love. Because validation is such an important need, it simply cannot be trusted to others alone. We each must be able to validate ourselves.

VALIDATION

It is very easy to fall into the trap of thinking your worth as a person comes from what you do instead of who you are. It is also easy to see your worth as being reflected off others instead of shining out from inside. When you allow other people or outside situations to provide your validation, you make yourself hostage to them.

When we validate ourselves, we recognize our worth. Notice I didn't say we *generate* our worth or *create* our worth or *cause* our worth. Each of us has a worth, a value that we did not generate, create, or cause for ourselves. This value is inherent in us as people; this value is a gift from God.

Each person is unique, looked over and loved by God. One of my favorite psalms in Scripture is Psalm 139 because it speaks of the intimate and loving relationship God has with each one of us. God knows us as individuals, not just as an anonymous blob in the mass of humanity. He knows our name and everything about us. Jesus in Luke 12:6–7 explains that we have great value to God and that "the very hairs of [our heads] are all numbered" (v. 7). Do you know yourself well enough to know how many hairs you have at any given time? This may seem like rhetorical hyperbole, but it is meant to illustrate that God, your loving Father, knows who you are.

God knows you and loves you, as you. Your value and worth as a person do not derive from what you do or who you're in relationship with. It doesn't spring out of how much money you make or how attractive you are or how many times you can get an answer right. Your value is deeply rooted in your identity in God. Genesis 1:27 clearly says that God made you in His image. You are, as Psalm 139:14 says, "fearfully and wonderfully made." This isn't talking about your mother's eyes or your father's ears. This is talking about that part of you that comes directly from God, who verse 13 says crafted your creation. God made you who you are and loves you for who you are. This is the bedrock foundation for self-worth. This is self-worth anchored in God; this is your special identity safe and protected in God's hands. You can validate yourself by recognizing your worth in Him.

There are times when it seems we have to stand alone and shout out our value to a deaf world. Those around us who should have joined in the chorus with loud and enthusiastic voices are either silent or murmuring a negative undercurrent. So often this happens when we're most vulnerable—as children. We take the silence of our parents or trusted adults as proof we are not worthy or special. We listen to their murmurs and turn up the volume until that din is all we can hear. Yet, deep in our hearts, we know this isn't true; we know deep in our hearts this is somehow wrong and unfair.

Sometimes we are taught that it's wrong to validate ourselves. Maybe you've been taught it's boastful or prideful to love yourself. I remember sitting in Bible classes as a child and learning I was supposed to love myself last on a list that went something like God, others, self. It was as if there was only so much love to go around, and you weren't supposed to hoard it for yourself but rather give up your supply of love for everyone else. If you had any left over for yourself it was because you hadn't given up enough to God or others.

I believe this is faulty reasoning. After all, doesn't God say that you are to "love your neighbor as yourself" (Lev. 19:18)? Galatians 5:14 says that the entire law of God is summed up in that single command. And didn't Paul in Ephesians 5:28–29 say that a man was to love his wife like he loved his own body, in the same way Christ loves His church? It seems to me that loving yourself is a fundamental principle of God. Loving yourself is not supposed to be subservient to the love of others; love of self is the basis for love of others. This is why it is so important to be able to validate yourself as a person, created and loved by God, with intrinsic value and worth just for who you are. Validation isn't something to be earned; it is something to be claimed.

As an adult, I know that love isn't a finite quantity. Love has no more boundaries and limitations than God does because God is love (1 John 4:8). Love is like the living water Jesus talked about to the woman at the well in John 4. There is an endless supply with plenty to go around.

Please know that God joins you in your validation. He's the author of your worth and value, so why shouldn't He shout it out with you? In *The Message,* Eugene Peterson translates Psalm 37:5–6 this way: "Open up before God, keep nothing back; he'll do whatever needs to be done. He'll validate your life in the clear light of day and stamp you with approval at high noon."

RECOGNIZE, ILLUSTRATE, AND ESTABLISH SELF-WORTH

We've talked about recognizing your worth as a person. That's just one of the components of validation. Validation also means to illustrate and establish. Your actions to yourself illustrate your sense of self-worth. What you say is one thing; what you do is another. How you treat yourself, the attitudes you have about yourself, the forgiveness you show yourself, the love you have for yourself illustrate what is really true. Once you recognize your value as a person, your need for the cheap clanging of outside excessities will fade. You need to illustrate that knowledge through action.

Planting Seeds

For those unfamiliar with this feeling of self-worth, you'll need to practice recognizing and establishing it. In order to help with this, I'd like you to write a story. This is to be a description of you—a story about you—written in the third person (using "he" or "she" instead of "I" and "me"). Be honest and truthful about how you feel about yourself. I'll include some space here for you to write a few paragraphs. As you're able, please feel free to either expand on other paper or use this as a springboard to write more in depth.

Description of _____:

As you think about what you've written, I'd like you to do the following:

Circle any descriptive terms you used about yourself.

Place a star next to any circled descriptive word that is positive.

Place a triangle next to any circled descriptive word that
is negative.

Count how many stars and how many triangles you have.
Which is greater—stars or triangles?

Look over the positive stars. For each one: Can you identify
when you first felt this way about yourself? Is it tied to a particular
time or event in your life? Is it tied to a particular person in your
life? This is a significant life moment. Close your eyes, and think
back to that time. Meditate on that life moment. You have recognized its importance; it is being illustrated in your mind as you
think about it; now establish it as a point of validation.

Look over the negative triangles. Before you do the same
thing as with the stars, I'd like you to reexamine the negative
descriptions you assigned yourself. Ask yourself whether or not
this is really true. For example, you may have written that you
are a selfish, judgmental person and identified this as a negative.
But is that really true? Do you recognize this negative in yourself,
or has someone said that you are selfish and judgmental? For
instance, if you're in relationship with an alcoholic and have asked
that person to stop drinking, she may have yelled that you are a
selfish, judgmental person out of her anger and desire to keep
drinking. It's important to really think about each of the negatives you put down and interrogate where they come from. So,
for each one: Can you identify when you first felt this way about
yourself? Is it tied to a particular time or event in your life? Is it
tied to a particular person in your life? Did you come to feel this

way about yourself on your own, or did others tell you that you were this way?

It's important to determine the basis for your negatives because some will be true and some will be false. Because you're a fallible person, you are going to have some negatives. *Having negatives does not negate your value as a person.* You do not need to be perfect in order to have value. God gave you your value even knowing how many times in life you'd mess up. Perfection is not the key that opens up God's box of value. Perfection is the brown wrapper keeping that gift hidden, always saying *not yet, not yet,* to your recognition of your value. Throw the wrapper away; open up the box.

It's important to identify the source of the false negatives. By recognizing them you become alert to them and can reject those negative thoughts and attitudes. Highlight them. Examine them. Figure out where they come from, and send them back where they belong. Refuse to cart them around any longer.

It's also important to recognize your true negatives. God gave us inherent value as human beings, and part of that value is our capacity to learn, change, and grow. Acting from a position of strength, recognizing your positives, you can begin a process of addressing and improving on your negatives. One of the most important values to a true negative is the opportunity it affords you to forgive yourself. So often, people turn away or hide from their true negatives because they are not anchored to their core worth as a person. The ability to recognize your faults, forgive yourself, love yourself, and learn is a real positive. It's an opportunity to hug yourself and say, "It's okay; I forgive you!"

As you practice self-validation and acknowledging your self-worth, accentuate your positives. Look over your positives again, thinking about the role they play in your life. How do you benefit from your positives? How do others? Thank God for them and celebrate them. This is not boasting; this is recognizing, and recognizing is part of validation.

Before I close this chapter, I'd like you go again to the verses that started it. They come from Psalm 22, which starts out "My God, my God, why have you forsaken me?" It is what Jesus cries out on the cross just before He dies. As you are able, I'd like you to read over this entire psalm. Written hundreds of years before Jesus arrived on earth, these words are a beautiful, gut-wrenching account of what Jesus felt as He died. For those of you who have been marginalized, mocked, and scorned by others, Jesus knows how you feel. For those of you who have questioned who you are because of how you've been treated, Jesus understands. He went through what He did so that you would know and understand the truth of His love, your value to Him, and your worth as a person. Jesus illustrated His love for you through His sacrifice on the cross. He established that love by His willingness to die for you. No one and nothing can shake His amazing love for you; it belongs to you. Take hold of it and let the rest go.

> *Father, I thank You that I am not a worm,*
> *even though I think others may see me as*
> *such. I thank You that I am fearfully and*
> *wonderfully made and that You know my*
> *name. When I listen to the murmurs of*

others, help me hear Your voice of love clearly. Help me recognize when I reach for other things or other people to validate me. Anchor my value and worth as a person firmly within You. By faith, I trust You to do this.

7

Our Need for Control

As Paul discoursed on righteousness, self-control and the judgment to come, Felix was afraid and said, "That's enough for now! You may leave. When I find it convenient, I will send for you." (Acts 24:25)

There is a wide difference between control and self-control. Many of us would admit to a desire for control in our lives and in fact have developed patterns and behaviors to attempt to achieve it. We're not as diligent, however, when it comes to incubating an environment as amenable to self-control. One of the reasons we want to have control globally is to let ourselves off the hook personally where self-control is involved: "If I can control the things and people around me, it makes it less imperative for me to control myself."

Control is a fascinating and frustrating paradox, especially in my line of work. The paradox I see comes when people start out engaging in some sort of behavior (including excessities) in an attempt to bring a sense of order and control into their lives. There comes a point, however, when the hunter becomes the hunted and the *Gotta*

Have It! turns on them. The very thing they invited into their lives to bring control now controls *them*.

TERI'S STORY

Teri thought she was an independent woman, but even in adulthood she lived in the shadows of her mother's angst. Teri's mother, preoccupied with her own weight issues, began to transfer that anxiety onto Teri as a child. It wasn't enough that her mother measured and fretted over everything she ate—she wanted to include Teri in her swirl of perpetual dieting, calorie counting, and nutrient mapping.

Somewhere around eleven or twelve years old, Teri decided to take control of her life. She figured out she didn't have a lot of ground to work with, given she was still living at home under her parents' strict rules. But, being an inventive adolescent, she began to find ways to assert herself. Teri rebelled by refusing to eat in her mother's presence whenever possible. It wasn't really that hard to do. Her mother was so busy getting ready for work in the morning that she never bothered to eat breakfast and rarely ventured into the kitchen for more than a hurried cup of coffee. Lunch was easy; Teri ate at school. Most evenings either she had things going on, or her mother did, so dinner together rarely coincided. On the weekends, she could usually get out of at least one evening meal by going to a friend's house. Sundays were the hardest because it meant a meal after church together, but Teri had gotten very good at eating slowly and pushing the food around her plate, outlasting her mother, who never seemed very comfortable at the dinner table.

Away from her mother, Teri ate whatever she wanted, in whatever quantity suited her. She relished eating the kinds of foods she knew her mother would cringe at—either because she would never consider eating them or because Teri suspected her mother really longed to eat them. Eating on her own, her way, became Teri's declaration of independence.

This worked pretty well through middle school, but in high school, things changed. Even though her mother rarely saw her eat, the effect of what she ate started to show. Teri began to gain weight. Comments from her mother expanded from what she ate to how she looked. One night while staying at a friend's house, Teri complained about this unwanted level of scrutiny. In the dark and quiet privacy of her friend's bedroom, Teri shared that she wanted to lose weight but was finding it hard. Then her friend described a way she could eat whatever she wanted and not gain weight. This was just what Teri was looking for. It seemed a fair trade—learning how and when to vomit up her food in order to still get to eat it. Now she could eat what she wanted and not have to deal with all the disadvantages of weight gain. She could still be in control.

Like so many others, Teri came to work with me after being bulimic over half her life. She wanted to stop but couldn't. She no longer had to force herself to vomit; instead, her stomach tended to heave up its contents without conscious effort. Teri admitted, "My life is out of control." What started out as a way for a teenager to take control ended up controlling her life as an adult.

I recognize that most of you reading Teri's story probably won't identify with the bulimia aspect. However, most of you should be able to connect with the *control* aspect. Maybe you haven't lost control to bulimia in your life. Maybe it's alcohol. Maybe it's acquiring stuff. Maybe it's cigarettes or prescription drugs. Maybe you can connect with the eating part of Teri's story. You started out doing whatever it is as a way to declare your independence, as a way to say you were perfectly capable of making your own choices, *thank you very much*. Somewhere, however, those choices turned into excessities and turned the tables on control. You thought that by choosing them you were exerting control over your life. Little did you know that you'd end up dependent upon them and that they'd control you.

THE POWER OF YES

Strangely, the way we often choose to demonstrate our sense of control is by our ability to say yes to something. We think that because we choose to engage in the activity, we show control over that activity. This often happens at the time children turn into teenagers and young adults. They think their "adulthood" is manifest in how many places and ways they get to say yes to things parents and other authority figures previously told them to say no to. With this mindset, teenagers and young adults will say yes to things like alcohol, cigarettes, drugs, and sex.

Gotta Have It! behaviors can be perfectly suited to this "yes" illusion of control. Saying yes after an extended period of saying no is a giddy, heady, exhilarating feeling. Saying yes can be sheer relief, especially if no is interpreted as deprivation.

Growing up, Denise was constantly told no. No, she couldn't have that toy. No, she couldn't have that candy. No, she couldn't have that dress. Her family wasn't poor; her father just ruled the family like that was the case. Denise got in trouble if she didn't turn out the lights when she left a room because "that costs money!" She couldn't calculate the times she heard things like "Money doesn't grow on trees" or "What am I? Made of money?" or "You can have that when you're old enough to buy it yourself." Her father, who seemed to resent how much money it took to raise his family, usually said these things in a raised voice. It was as if he went around in a state of shock over the cost of things, and that shock generally got translated into irritation, frustration, and anger.

As far as Denise could tell, he didn't keep the money to pay for personal extravagances. He was as austere with his own life as he demanded of everyone else. It wasn't that he wanted more for himself, Denise came to believe, but that he didn't want it for anyone. When she realized that's the way he was, Denise began to take it personally. She decided the issue wasn't really about the money—it was about control. Her father controlled money as a way to control her and the rest of the family. Over time, her resentment grew.

Fortunately Denise was able to get a scholarship to help with tuition in college, along with student loans, because her father would never have paid for any of it. But she was smart and landed a good job after college. Having paychecks with her name on them made Denise feel liberated. This was her money; she earned it. Nobody else had a right to tell her what to do with it. She developed a love of high-end purses and shoes, sunglasses and jewelry. She furnished her apartment with the latest furniture in the current color palette. She reveled in the ability to hand her credit card over. It was her way of saying yes, and it felt marvelous.

Marvelous, that is, until Denise began to have difficulty even meeting the minimum monthly payments on her collection of credit cards. A friend at work casually asked if she'd ever considered putting together a budget. Even the word sounded distasteful. That's all Denise remembered growing up: how all of them were supposed to be living within "the budget." Every end of the month, as she sweated and worried about being able to pay her bills, Denise promised that the very next month she'd start saying no to things and get her spending under control. That's all she needed to do, just get her spending under control.

Of course, to get her spending under control she'd have to get herself under control first.

THE POWER OF NO

So many people hit their young-adult years believing control is all about saying yes to those things they were previously denied. I think it takes us a bit longer to figure out that often the best way to exhibit our control is by choosing to say no to those same things. I guess you could call this the difference between control and self-control. So often we think control is about *finally* making sure we get what we want. Self-control, however, is more about making sure we get what we need.

Self-control is not easy to come by, requiring the long view over instant gratification and initially appearing harsh, unpleasant, and virtually impossible to employ. It requires practice, patience, and perseverance. Self-control presupposes an intimate knowledge of self, knowing what is and is not good and appropriate for you. It's that person at the buffet who is able to cheerfully say, "No, thank you," to that big piece of chocolate layer cake (when you've gone back for seconds). It's the oddity of someone who is able to say no to thirty more minutes of sleep in order to get up to jog in the rain and the cold (when it's all you can do to crawl out of bed thirty minutes late). It's the anomaly of the person who is able to put down work and go home at the end of the day, saying no to the urge to stay another hour (when you consistently find yourself—once again—being the last one in the office to lock up). Self-control is that and so much more.

Self-control in Scripture is interesting and sometimes amusing. Here are some examples from the Old Testament that talk about what happens when you have self-control and what happens when you don't:

> Better a patient man than a warrior, a man
> who controls his temper than one who
> takes a city. (Prov. 16:32)

The warrior says yes to battle while the patient man says wait. Being able to control your temper can be more of a triumph than engaging in the battle.

> Like a city whose walls are broken down is
> a man who lacks self-control. (Prov. 25:28)

Self-control is a valuable defense against all kinds of problems. If you lack it, you leave yourself wide open and vulnerable.

> A fool gives full vent to his anger, but a
> wise man keeps himself under control.
> (Prov. 29:11)

Giving full vent to anger or any *Gotta Have It!* excessity rarely produces the fruit you expect or projects you in a positive light. Anger may get you what you want, but it robs you of what you need, especially in relationships.

The New Testament is certainly not silent where self-control is involved. It is listed as one of the fruit of the Spirit in Galatians 5:22–23. Its value is recognized and affirmed in 1 Thessalonians 5:6 and 8. Leaders in the church are to be self-controlled (1 Tim. 3:2; Titus 1:8; 2:5). Self-control is valued across the age spectrum (Titus 2:2, 6). Each person is instructed to exercise self-control (1 Peter 1:13; 4:7; 5:8).

THE OTHER IN SELF-CONTROL

It is obvious that self-control is a virtue and a value. It can also, sadly, be in very short supply in life. You know it is good. You want to be able to exercise control over self. None of us want to admit we aren't able to control ourselves. So how do you develop a better grasp of saying no? The answer, of course, lies within each person—and outside of each person. In the paradoxical way of Scripture, one way to control self lies completely outside of self. The work certainly is within you, but your help and your hope to gain and mature in this self-control, thankfully, are not totally up to you. Titus 2:11–13 says, "For the grace of God that brings salvation has appeared to all men. It teaches us to say 'No' to ungodliness and worldly passions, and to live self-controlled, upright and godly lives in this present age, while we wait for the blessed hope—the glorious appearing of our great God and Savior, Jesus Christ."

Self-control, then, is a gift of God—not some divine *zap* but rather a process taught by God. Self-control is your control over self, but it's a joint effort between you and God. We, frankly, need help in this department. The Bible says this: "I obviously need help! I realize that I don't have what it takes. I can will it, but I can't do it. I decide to do good, but I don't really do it; I decide not to do bad, but then I do it anyway…. Something has gone wrong deep within me and gets the better of me every time" (Rom. 7:17–20 MSG).

Taken individually, many of the *Gotta Have It!* behaviors we've talked about aren't bad or wrong. Our excessities go wrong when they get the better of us every time, when they are in control, not us. The only way to get back control is to develop and strengthen our self-control. When dealing with our excessities, we need to ask, "Who's in charge?"

WHO'S IN CHARGE?

As human beings, we want to be in control of our own lives. This is a universal characteristic, whether people profess faith or not. Control is interpreted as freedom, while loss of control is interpreted as slavery. The paradox is that we invite excessities into our lives from our position of control. We use our control and decide to engage in the *Gotta Have It!* behavior.

Excessities, however, are notoriously bad guests. They don't tend to stay within the boundaries we set. Once told yes, they don't like to be told no, and they perpetually promise what they can't deliver. Before long, what you invited into your life to obey your needs ends up becoming the one you obey. The sad reality is we begin excessities thinking they will be our slaves—to bring us significance or value or pleasure or numbness whenever we decide—but they end up enslaving us.

Perhaps one of the most insightful groups into this phenomenon of control and slavery and how one can turn into the other rather quickly is Alcoholics Anonymous. The alcoholic doesn't take that first drink thinking it's going to take over his or her life. No one forces them to take that first drink or the second or maybe even the third. After that, however, it gets a little murky. Alcoholism is a very slippery slope, and Alcoholics Anonymous bands together people in sobriety with a Twelve-Step path to recovery. Here are those Twelve Steps. As you read them, I'd like you to think in the context of your *Gotta Have It!* behavior, whether it's alcohol or not:

1. We admitted we were powerless over alcohol—
    that our lives had become unmanageable.

2. Came to believe that a Power greater than ourselves could restore us to sanity.

3. Made a decision to turn our will and our lives over to the care of God as we understood Him.

4. Made a searching and fearless moral inventory of ourselves.

5. Admitted to God, to ourselves, and to another human being the exact nature of our wrongs.

6. Were entirely ready to have God remove all these defects of character.

7. Humbly asked Him to remove our shortcomings.

8. Made a list of all persons we had harmed, and became willing to make amends to them all.

9. Made direct amends to such people wherever possible, except when to do so would injure them or others.

10. Continued to take personal inventory and when we were wrong promptly admitted it.

11. Sought through prayer and meditation to improve our conscious contact with God, as we understood Him, praying only for knowledge of His will for us and the power to carry that out.

12. Having had a spiritual awakening as a result of these Steps, we tried to carry this message to

alcoholics, and to practice these principles in all
our affairs.[1]

The Twelve Steps, especially the first three, speak to a very fundamental reality that is constantly misconstrued and overlooked: first,
that when our lives become unmanageable, they are out of control; and
second, that in order to get back control, we have to completely give up
control. Jesus puts it this way: "For whoever wants to save his life will
lose it, but whoever loses his life for me will save it" (Luke 9:24). Again,
self-control isn't something you can arrive at all on your own. Rather,
you gain self-control when you give it up to something else.

Giving up control is a frightening prospect for many people. They
believe the control they have is the only thing holding the monsters of
life at bay. What they don't realize is that this control isn't opening the
door to freedom; it's keeping the door closed with them imprisoned
inside. The monsters aren't being kept on the other side of the door;
the monsters are really on their side of the door, being kept in. Teri
thought she was in control of her weight and her self-esteem by engaging in bulimia. For years she resisted change because she strongly felt
that, even as bad as it was sometimes, life would be worse without it.
Denise thought once she became an adult and was in control of her
life she could buy whatever she wanted, whenever she wanted. For
years she resisted change because saying no to herself always sounded
like her father's voice. As difficult as their lives were, each somehow felt
that at least it was "her" life and that she was in control. They believed
engaging in those behaviors was building up and maintaining a wall
of protection around them when, in reality, their walls were breached
by those behaviors.

GIVE UP TO GAIN

As topsy-turvy and scary as it sounds, the best way to gain control is to give it up. You need to understand an important point: The control you are so hesitant to give up is in reality not *your* control; it is the control the excessity has *over you*. This is a tug-of-war of wills—yours versus the excessity. In order to wrest control back, you need to call in reinforcements. You need to give up your control, as the AA second step says, to a Power greater than yourself.

As those in Alcoholics Anonymous have learned, there is a greater Power than yourself. He is ready, willing, and able to help you gain control in your life over your excessities. However, you have to trust Him and submit to Him. Psalm 32:8–9 says, "I will instruct you and teach you in the way you should go; I will counsel you and watch over you. Do not be like the horse or the mule, which have no understanding but must be controlled by bit and bridle or they will not come to you." Horses and mules do not naturally obey, so people control them with bits and bridles. The person without self-control is like a horse or a mule that must obey the will of whoever or whatever controls the bit and bridle. You've lived a life under the bit and bridle of your excessity. Isn't it time to throw off that earthly rein and submit yourself to a divine one?

Planting Seeds

For this section, I'd like you to think about the progression your excessity takes. It might look something like this:

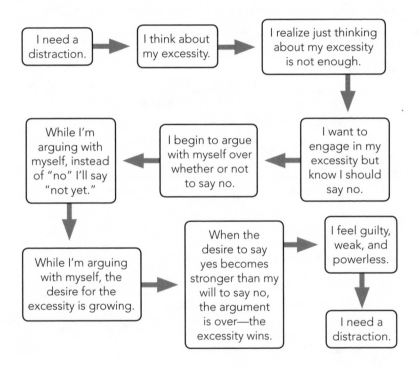

Now, I'd like you to write out your own progression to excessity:

1.

2.

3.

4.

5.

6.

7.

8.

9.

10.

11.

12.

You may or may not have twelve steps. The number isn't important; the content of those steps is. Looking over the ones I provided for example, obviously, these steps do not contain the victory of those of AA. My steps are all about submitting to the excessity, while the AA steps are all about submitting to God. Big difference. I'd like you to look over your steps and compare them to the steps of AA.

How are they different?

How are they similar?

Again, I am not saying your excessity is a sin, but it might be helpful in this discussion to look at the progression of sin talked about in James 1:12–15:

> Blessed is the man who perseveres under trial, because when he has stood the test, he will receive the crown of life that God has promised to give to those who love him.
>
> When tempted, no one should say, "God is tempting me." For God cannot be tempted by evil, nor does he tempt anyone; but each one is tempted when, by his own evil desire, he is dragged away and enticed. Then, after the desire has conceived, it gives birth to sin; and sin, when it is full-grown, gives birth to death.

Here is what I get out of this passages, in regard to excessities:

Saying no to an excessity is a trial and requires perseverance.

Turning over control of your excessity to God shows you love Him.

Excessities are very good at blaming other people and things and using that blame to justify their existence.

We open the door to excessities by our desire for what they bring to our lives.

When we give in to these desires, we give control of our lives to the excessity.

With the excessity in control, the quality of our lives is degraded.

The more we say yes to the excessity, the more we say no to life.

Next, I'd like you to rewrite the AA Twelve Steps, just for yourself and your excessity. If you have more than one excessity, I'd like you to pick the one you feel you are ready to address. Once you have worked through the steps for that excessity, you'll have encouragement and motivation to begin with another, and then another, until you are actively in recovery for each. As you work through your excessity and the steps, if there is an assignment that needs to be done for a particular step, like step four, please do it. Use what you've already done in this book as a springboard.

My Excessity Twelve Steps:

1.

2.

3.

4.

5.

6.

7.

8.

9.

10.

11.

12.

Doing this exercise will not be easy. It is a trial and will require patience and perseverance. As you walk through this trial, I especially want you to pay attention to your self-talk, the arguments you carry on with yourself. Be aware of each argument, rationale, and excuse that surfaces. As you are able, begin to counter those arguments with what you know from Scripture. If your knowledge isn't where you want it to be, spend time reading the Word. Ask God to point out passages and promises that directly counter the arguments that have been so effective in the past. Ask Him to give you ammunition to blow apart your "thought bubbles." Write these down. Post them on your refrigerator, your bathroom mirror, the dashboard of your car. Memorize them. Say them out loud to yourself as you're driving or walking down the road.

Whenever the excessity urge hits, marshal your resources, because you can be sure your excessity is bringing to bear everything available to overwhelm your best intentions. Above all, actively work to turn over your will to God's where your excessity is involved. It is not in God's will for you to be enslaved by anything except righteousness (see Romans 6). It is not in God's will for you to be controlled by anything other than His Spirit. And Romans 8:6b promises that "the mind controlled by the Spirit is life and peace." This is the victory God so longs to give you. The world says to horde control. God says give up control. The world cautions you to trust no one. God whispers to trust in Him. Given what you know and have experienced with both of those paths, I urge you to choose God.

> *Father God, You've asked me to give up my life in order to keep it. You've asked me to cede control in order to experience it. I confess these don't always make sense, especially when the world is clamoring in my ears. I am so afraid of what will happen if I give up control, even in the face of the mess it's brought to my life. Give me peace and courage to find my control in You and not myself. When*

I'm losing my own argument, speak for me, advocate for me, defend me against myself. Give me hope each day.

Section 3

What God Provides

I remember stopping by the playroom at church one Sunday after services on my way to pick up my youngest, who was not yet able to sit quietly through the worship service. As I stopped to talk with another parent by the door, our conversation was abruptly halted by the shrill scream of one of the two children still left in the playroom. It was one of those indignant, high-pitched yells that makes the hairs on the back of your neck stand straight up.

Both of us immediately jerked our heads back toward the room to see what was wrong. The toddler who was crying so profusely had an armful of toys she'd picked up and was holding on to for dear life. She didn't appear hurt. There was no one around her. There was, however, another child in the opposite corner of the room, with a single toy. Red faced and livid, the crying child dropped all of the toys she had and made a beeline for the other child and the other toy.

I think we're kind of like that toddler when it comes to what God provides. We have been given an absolute armload full of blessings and gifts from God. But instead of appreciating or even paying attention to what we've been given, we often pitch a fit and drop everything to run after the one thing we want.

8

God Provides Patience

Through patience a ruler can be persuaded, and
a gentle tongue can break a bone. (Prov. 25:15)

In today's society, we have come to expect the instantaneous, the rapid, the quick, the get-it-done-right-now. We are simply impatient people. We used to have a higher capacity for patience, but it keeps getting whacked off—primarily as a result of advances in technology. Cell phones, email, texting, and twittering create their own expectation momentum. What used to be considered just waiting now must be endured with patience. Patience really means *being put off.* Nobody likes being put off.

Excessities are at war with patience. The *Gotta Have It!* cry of an excessity is generally followed by the unspoken command of *Now!* The longer you are required to wait, the louder that command becomes until it's so shrill that it's all you hear. The internal clamor of the excessity creates its own urgency. What was a desire becomes a necessity. And a necessity deferred becomes an emergency. Once you've declared your own emergency, you have provided built-in justification for whatever measures are required to satisfy your *Gotta*

Have It! At this point, patience is a hindrance, a barrier between you and your excessity.

LORI'S STORY

Lori didn't like barriers to what she wanted. She never had. Because she saw what she wanted so clearly and perceived her need so acutely, she took barriers personally. Her family learned it was never a good idea to get between Lori and something she wanted. They tended to scatter whenever she was in one of her "moods." Her work subordinates learned to keep their heads down, their mouths shut, and their hands busy doing whatever Lori wanted. Capable and driven, Lori was able to accomplish a great deal in a small amount of time. It was something she was known for and something she took a great deal of pride in.

If you asked Lori, she'd say she had a great deal of patience. She would relate numerous occasions where she'd patiently endured the incompetence, inattention, and lack of caring of people around her. She could be patient long enough for the microwave to heat up her food. She could be patient long enough for her computer to boot up. She could be patient long enough for her gas tank to fill. These were Lori's ideas of patience, and she bore them with stoic, if resentful, patience.

Then the ground underneath Lori shifted. Her husband was diagnosed with cancer, and Lori learned she really wasn't patient after all. Cancer taught her how to wait. She had to wait for test results to be done. She had to wait for doctors and medical personnel to do their work. She had to wait for her husband's strength to return after each agonizing round of chemotherapy or radiation. She had to wait for hope to return after each setback.

When it became clear he would not recover, Lori had a decision to make. Before, Lori had always traded time for results. Now, the only result time would yield was the loss of her husband. Before, Lori couldn't wait for life to move fast enough. Now, all she wanted to do was slow it down. Before, whatever was happening right now in Lori's life was overshadowed by what could or would happen in the future, with what needed to be done. Lori's life before was a relentless race from the now to the next.

With the next thing being the impending death of her husband, Lori's life came to an abrupt halt. She cut back at work so she could spend more time with him. As a result, she spent more time with her children, who desperately needed her. It was impossible for her to stop the clock, to slow the progression of the disease, to keep her husband alive longer. So instead, Lori learned to wring every possible drop of value and joy out of each moment they were together. She stopped being resentful of time and began to live within it. Before, Lori had always lived impatiently for what she wanted. Now, she learned to live patiently for what she didn't.

THE TRUTH ABOUT PATIENCE

Through her husband's cancer, Lori learned she wasn't in control. She learned that life sometimes throws you situations or circumstances that are simply beyond your control. She learned that it doesn't matter how competent, how motivated, how used to being in charge you are—sometimes you aren't in charge. She learned that sometimes the only option is to be patient.

The world does not see patience as a position of strength but rather as a position of weakness, of wanting, of lack. Powerful people don't have to wait; powerless people do. This is a fundamental misunderstanding of patience. Patience allows you to take back control over a capricious and unstable world and plant that control firmly within yourself. Patience does not give you the power over circumstances; patience allows you to control yourself in the midst of circumstances.

Patience, as an attitude, has been misunderstood. Because of the misconceptions I've run into over the years as I've helped people develop the capacity for patience in their lives, I'd like to go over some of the realities and truths of patience.

Patience is not apathy. Apathy is a lack of interest or concern. Being patient does not mean disengaging or disconnecting from your feelings or emotions. Being patient means accepting both how you feel about a given situation and what you can realistically do about it.

Patience is not surrender. A decision to exercise patience is not the equivalent of waving the white flag. When you surrender, you place yourself under the control of the situation and remove yourself from the equation. Patience is not surrendering your power to the circumstance; patience is redeploying that power back to you.

Patience is not static. There is a misconception that patience, or the act of waiting, is just sitting there, doing nothing. In this, patience is a little like sleep. When we're sleeping, it can appear that we're doing nothing—we're just sleeping. Sleep, however, is a highly dynamic process where the body is actively engaged in repairing itself. The mind is filtering and collating and processing the events of the day. In the same way, patience is an active time of remembering, reexamining, and recommitting to those things you know are true. Patience, like sleep, is the act of preparing for the new day to come.

Patience is not impossible. One of the biggest lies of your excessity is that you must give in to it right now. This lie says you do not have the capacity to be patient and to wait—and it would be foolish to even try.

Patience is optimistic expectation. The engine of patience is hope. Romans 5:3–4 is a wonderful passage that shows the connection between patience and hope: "Not only so, but we also rejoice in our sufferings, because we know that suffering produces perseverance; perseverance, character; and character, hope." In this case, the patience piece is called perseverance. So, in that odd paradoxical way of Scripture, if you can hang in there despite the negative, you'll arrive at the ultimate positive: hope. Apathy says, *Give up; there is no hope.* Patience says, *Stick with it; there is reason to hope.* You cannot be patient if you've given up all hope, because there would be nothing to be patient for.

Patience is based on the end, not the beginning. Ecclesiastes 7:8 says, "The end of a matter is better than its beginning, and patience is better than pride." You won't know that the end of the matter is better than the beginning if you're not patient enough to get there. Beginnings are often events full of pride—we've started; we've set our course. How often, though, do we begin something full of pride but fail to stick with it to completion? Pride may motivate us to start, but patience gives us the endurance to see it through to the better end.

Patience is based on the long view. The view of patience is not a few steps in front of us. The view of patience is out over the horizon, around the bend, through the hills and valleys of life. Patience is not thwarted by the immediate; it is sustained by the eventual. When you are assured of the eventual, you can patiently endure the immediate.

Patience is a wise response to life. This life is offensive in so many ways. People can be mean, cruel, and hurtful. Circumstances can be sudden, unpredictable, and damaging. We may feel as if we live under siege from something or someone most of the time. In response, you could go around getting angry and engaging in battle over every slight, every injury, every unfair circumstance. I have known people who do. They are usually exhausted, full of anger, and quick to explode. They are generally not very patient. But remaining in full battle mode is not a wise way to live your life. It produces incredible stress, alienates the people around you, and distorts your ability to enjoy and appreciate life. Patience provides a calm counterbalance to the frenzy of such a threat level. Proverbs 19:11 says, "A man's wisdom gives him patience; it is to his glory to overlook an offense." Angry people rarely pass up the opportunity to make full use of an offense. Patient people are wise enough to overlook it.

Patience is a calm response to life. As I said above, patience provides a calm counterbalance to the attack-mode stance toward life. Patience is seen as a way to diffuse tension and calm an emotional storm. Proverbs 14:29 says, "A patient man has great understanding, but a quick-tempered man displays folly." And as Proverbs 15:18 says, "A hot-tempered man stirs up dissension, but a patient man calms a quarrel." Excessities are often quick to strike within tense situations. They promise relief and reward in the midst of such emotional storms. Patience has a way of de-escalating the situation and reducing the pull of escape into an excessity.

Patience is an acquired trait. We are not born patient. Patience is something we need to grow into. It is a character trait learned through life experiences. Of course, many of us do not choose to acquire this trait. Those who fail to learn patience, however, are destined to continue to find themselves in situations where they'll need it. The wise thing to do would be to learn the lesson, because trials and problems won't change. The only thing you can truly change is yourself. Eugene Peterson puts James 1:2–4 this way: "Consider it a sheer gift, friends, when tests and challenges come at you from all sides. You know that under pressure, your faith-life is forced into the open and shows its true colors. So don't try to get out of anything prematurely. Let it do its work so you become mature and well-developed, not deficient in any way" (MSG).

ACCEPTING THE GIFT

Patience is a gift from God. We want the gift of patience, but often our problem is that we're not really thrilled with how it's packaged. Patience comes wrapped inside trials and hardships.

God's gift of patience is one He expects you to unwrap and use. I believe one of the reasons is because He knows it's such a practical gift. We're going to need it for ourselves, for our relationships with others, for our relationship with God, and for just walking around in this world. Patience is God's gift, but it comes with an expectation of use and practice—God gives us the gift and then graciously puts us into situations where we'll need to use it.

Patience is especially useful when it comes to another word we're not overly fond of in our own lives: *change*. Change is process; it is the act of turning something that was one way into something different. Generally, these sorts of miracles do not take place overnight, no matter what the late-night infomercials say. Change requires patience because change takes time.

Change can be an unsettling process, often involving emotional, physical, and spiritual heavy lifting. It is hard and slow, so patience is required. God expects us to change. He wants us to change. He wants us to move from where we are now to where He wants us to be. He wants us to exhibit patience in the process, just as He exhibits patience with us. Not only is patience a gift; it is also a responsibility. How responsible are you with patience in your life? God gives you patience, but He is expecting a return on His investment.

In Colossians, the apostle Paul speaks of the responsibility we have because of our relationship with God:

> And we pray this in order that you may live a life worthy of the Lord and may please him in every way: bearing fruit in every good work, growing in the knowledge of God, being strengthened with all power according to his glorious might so that you may have great endurance and patience, and joyfully giving thanks to the Father, who has qualified you to share in the inheritance of the saints in the kingdom of light. (1:10–12)

God gives you all power not so that you'll be all-powerful and avoid problems. Instead, He wants you to experience great endurance, patience, and joy in the midst of the problems.

God expects us to be patient with ourselves, with others, and with Him. In all my years of counseling, this is perhaps one of the most difficult spiritual attributes to possess: patience with God. When Christians undergo severe hardship, trauma, and illness, there is a natural tendency to cry out to God and ask, "Why?" This is usually not a patient question at the time it is uttered. It is an anguished, heartfelt demand-request for an answer—an immediate answer. For many of these questions, the answers are not immediately forthcoming. For many, waiting and patience are involved.

But hope is involved as well. If you are waiting for an answer from God, for the "whys" in your life, you need patience and you need hope—patience to endure today and hope to believe in tomorrow. Yours is the cry of King David in Psalm 40:1–3: "I waited patiently for the LORD; he turned to me and heard my cry. He lifted me out of the slimy pit, out of the mud and mire; he set my feet on a rock and gave me a firm place to stand. He put a new song in my mouth, a hymn of praise to our God. Many will see and fear and put their trust in the LORD."

It is important to remember that even though God lifted David out of the pit, He didn't put him there in the first place. Some people blame God for the pits in their lives. They believe that because God is all-powerful, any pit they fall into is ultimately God's fault because He could have prevented it if He wanted to. They have no patience with God because they blame Him for their circumstances in the first place.

God calls us to be patient even when He doesn't answer. Psalm 37:7 says, "Be still before the LORD and wait patiently for him." I have known people who have waited years, decades even, to finally receive the answer from God for what has happened in their lives. In the midst of their pain and confusion, they were called to trust God enough to be still before Him and wait for His answer. They hoped for an answer even when it didn't come. They lived out Romans 8:24–25, which says, "But hope that is seen is no hope at all. Who hopes for what he already has? But if we hope for what we do not yet have, we wait for it patiently." In hope, they waited patiently on God.

This is the kind of faith-life James was talking about. This is when your faith-life is tested and shows its true colors. Again, James says, "Be patient, then, brothers, until the Lord's coming. See how the farmer waits for the land to yield its valuable crop and how patient he is for the autumn and spring rains. You too, be patient and stand firm, because the Lord's coming is near" (5:7–8).

Planting Seeds

I'd like you to think about how patient a person you are. Go over the following situations, and think about how you would react. Take a minute to jot down a couple of sentences, explaining what first comes to your mind:

1. You're standing in line at the grocery store, and someone inadvertently moves in front of you. Do you ask that person to get in line behind you?

2. You're waiting at a stoplight. As the light turns green, the car in front of you just sits there. Do you wait for the driver to notice the green light, or do you honk your horn? If you honk your horn, how long do you wait before you do so?

3. You're out with a group of friends when your spouse makes a comment about you in passing that hurts your feelings. Do you confront your spouse immediately in front of the others? Do you wait until you're alone in the car driving home to bring it up? Do you decide to let it go and not bring it up at all?

4. You're watching your favorite television show when a family member enters the room and engages you in conversation. Do you ask that person to wait until a commercial?

5. You're in a meeting at work, and one of your coworkers is giving a presentation. As far as you're concerned, it's taking her twice as long to make her point as it would take you. Do you interrupt and move the presentation along?

6. You're in the grocery store and see an old acquaintance. The two of you start talking, but the other person monopolizes the conversation, talking only about what he's doing, and doesn't ask you any questions about yourself or your family. Do you cut the conversation short?

7. You've made a decision to lose some weight. Each morning you wake up expecting to see ever-lower numbers, but it's taking a lot longer than you thought. Do you just decide it's a lost cause and forget the whole thing?

8. You've been working with your eight-year-old on becoming more responsible. You've given her the task of helping you clean up after dinner. She comes to you and says she's through, but the salt and pepper shakers are still on the table, there are crumbs on the countertops, and the dirty place mats haven't been taken to the washer. Do you accept the job she's done, or do you say something? If you say something, how do you say it?

9. You've lost your job. You're doing all you can to find one, and you've been praying daily to God about finding work. Weeks go by with more résumés than interviews, and you still haven't gotten a job. Do you find yourself praying more or less?

Looking over your responses, would you say you reacted in a patient way or in an impatient way? Next to the number, write either "P" for patient or "I" for impatient.

For those you designated with a "P," write down what you think allows you to have patience in that circumstance. Is it something you learned growing up? Have you been on the opposite end of the situation and know how the other person feels? Is it just something that doesn't really push your patience button? Whatever it is, write it down.

Now, go back over the situations you marked with an "I" for impatient. Write down what emotions you feel when you put yourself in that scenario. Do you feel angry, frustrated, irritated, put upon, disrespected? What is it that shortens your patience fuse? How is your impatience demonstrated? Do you yell at the person, walk away, become aggressive?

Those nine scenarios were ones that I've come up with. I'd like you to write three of your own scenarios where you find yourself the least able to be patient. These should be situations where you know you *should* be patient but are not. Once you've written them down, I'd like you to explain the emotions you felt within each scenario and how you demonstrate impatience. If you have difficulty coming up with any, think about your everyday dealings with a spouse, family, or friends or certain situations.

I am impatient when:

1.

2.

3.

Now, go back to any of my nine you marked with an "I," and continue with your three, thinking about how you could act differently and be more patient in that situation. Look for Patience Patterns—these are things you can do to help strengthen your ability to be patient.

To help with this, allow me to let you know what my Patience Patterns are:

1. I don't take it personally. When I can realistically evaluate what is happening around me and not take it personally, the more patient I can be with my response. When I don't allow myself to feel personally attacked, it's much easier for me to respond in a calm and patient manner.

2. I take a deep breath and physically relax. Often, I channel tension through my body without realizing it. This tension can demand a physical release even if I'm not aware of it. If I can take a moment and diffuse that tension, I allow my body to relax. When I'm more relaxed, it's easier to exhibit patience.

3. I make a mental note. This one may just be me, but I'm always making mental notes about interesting reactions I have to things. If I make a mental note of an odd reaction, I give myself permission to defer it until a later time. This allows me to be patient in the current situation because I know I'll get back to processing it later.

4. I put myself in the other person's position. This is most helpful when I'm dealing with my kids. Sometimes I can get pretty impatient with their childish behavior. That is, of course, until I put myself in their position

and realize they're children—they're supposed to be childish. Stepping out of myself is a great way to see the larger picture and be more patient.

5. I pray. Sometimes I'm impatient when I think my time is being wasted. I'm a fairly busy person, so time is precious to me. As much as I try to orchestrate events, however, sometimes I just find myself in a holding pattern of some kind. In order not to become incensed and impatient, I find it very helpful to consider the unavoidable delay an opportune time to talk to God. That way, I've turned "down" time into "God" time.

Okay, now it's your turn. What are your Patience Patterns? My Patience Patterns:

1.

2.

3.

4.

5.

You're going to need your Patience Patterns. You're welcome to mine as well! The gift of patience is a hands-on experience from God. In order to grow and mature in patience, you're going to need to exercise it. So, I'd like you to begin to put your Patience Patterns into practice with your excessities. Use your Patience Patterns to put off saying yes to one excessity. Don't beat yourself up if you're initially unable to say no altogether. What I'd like you to do is practice your Patience Patterns in order to say "not yet" longer and longer. The goal is to put off giving in to your chosen excessity long enough that its power over you dissipates and you're able to say no. Pay attention to what your excessity is telling you during the time you defer giving in to it. Become aware of the arsenal of excuses, fears, anxieties, and rationales your excessity has mustered against you. Write them down. Remind yourself that these are false reasons, meant to keep you from realizing your full patience potential.

Be patient with yourself, but remember that giving in isn't being patient—it is capitulating; it is surrender. Keep yourself active and engaged, working toward your goal, not surrendering but continually gathering the power you've given to the excessity back to yourself. Ask God to be with you. Actively request to be strengthened in your patience.

> *Father, I know You are patient with me. I know I need to develop a greater ability to be patient in my own life. Help me quiet the clamor of the immediate so I can hear Your voice and rest in the peace of Your patience. Help me put my trust and confidence in You, even when I can't*

hear Your answers or see Your solutions.
Hold me close to You, even when I fail to
feel Your touch. Be patient with me.

9

God Provides Endurance

*I have fought the good fight, I have finished
the race, I have kept the faith. (2 Tim. 4:7)*

Excessities are, by nature, a here-and-now phenomenon. They are tied to the needs, wants, desires, anxieties, pleasures, and concerns of this life. But there's more to you and me than just the here and now; there is a hereafter waiting for us. Who wouldn't want to be able to say the same thing as the apostle Paul—that we'd fought the good fight, finished the race, kept the faith? This is a statement of victorious completion. It is a statement of confidence and peace.

Saying the statement is one thing; living the statement is quite another. What is implied in this statement is there was a fight going on; there were the possibility of not finishing and the potential of losing something vital. The statement is rock solid; the experience it's based on, upon reflection, appears somewhat precarious. The experience it's based on is called *life*.

In the last chapter, we looked at patience. In this chapter, we'll consider the role of endurance when it comes to victory over your excessities. It takes endurance to be able to make Paul's statement. In the midst of struggle, patience is what you have and endure is what you do.

Endurance is an interesting word. It means to undergo even something unpleasant without giving in. It means to accept or tolerate even something irritating. It means to continue in the same state, such as a monument enduring for centuries. It means to remain steady without yielding even under suffering.

When I think of endurance, I think of long-distance running. I think of a runner at the end of the race, breathing hard, sweaty and tired. If you've had to endure, you know you've been through something long and difficult. I think most people would agree that running, especially distance running, requires endurance. What you might not realize, however, is that while running requires endurance, it also *provides* it.

I started running several years back, and I've kept up with it, even as situations in my life have changed. When I first started running, I was dismayed at how quickly my body would tire. I couldn't gulp in air fast enough; even going a short distance was a test of endurance. But, as I kept up with it, I got better. I could go longer distances more easily. Running required my endurance, but it also increased my endurance. I used endurance to gain even more.

Whether or not you've articulated it as such, you're in a race. It's going to take endurance to get over your excessities, to turn down the volume on your *Gotta Have It!* demands. At first it will seem like turning aside from that desire takes all the energy you've got in your body and that saying no will leave you breathless. This is a battle of the wills—yours against the excessity. You will need endurance to undergo without giving in, to stay firm without yielding.

STEVE'S STORY

When Steve first came to counseling, he was losing the race and about to give up. His battle was a secret one, a contest of wills that threatened to overwhelm his life and drown him in shame. Steve's excessity, his *Gotta Have It!* activity, was Internet pornography. At first, he thought he could outrun his enemy. He was very careful about when he accessed the pornography and how much he allowed himself to indulge. He kept one step ahead by always blaming someone or something else for the push to porn. His wife provided an almost endless supply of reasons, real or imagined. The stresses at work and the foibles of life billowed the sails of his excuses and kept him out in front of his excessity, or so he thought.

What Steve failed to realize was the relentless nature of his *Gotta Have It!* It grew stronger and began to intrude into other areas of his life. Images and feelings once relegated to secret settings began to surface and interrupt and complicate his day. The pull of the pornography began to take him further and further away from his wife and his family.

After a close call at work, where using company computers to view pornography was grounds for immediate termination, Steve realized his excessity was controlling him. It appalled him that it was his fear of losing his job—not the betrayal of his marriage or the damage to his relationships, especially with his teenage daughters—that finally woke him up to how close he was to losing it all. He realized how out of balance his life had become, and he knew he needed to make a change. He knew what he wanted the ending to be; he just didn't realize how much he'd have to endure in the middle.

Steve had to endure his wife's moment of discovery and the subsequent devastation and loss of trust. He had to endure the physical and psychological drive to return to the pornography. He had to endure the realization that he was not as in control of himself as he'd always taken pride in. He had to endure peeling back the layers of his false assumptions, unmet desires, and selfish excuses in order to refute the lies and deceptions of the excessity. Simply put, Steve had to endure *exposure*. For a private and personal man, this was hard. At one point, he almost gave up, rebelling against any outside accountability to his behavior.

He almost gave up—but he didn't. When he thought he couldn't say no one more time or withstand the growing pressure to succumb to his excessity, he did. When he thought he couldn't stomach one more intrusion into the privacy of his past and present life, he did. When he thought he couldn't endure one more moment of vulnerability, he did. He endured and refused to yield. Steve found his second wind in the race against pornography.

FOOD THAT SPOILS

Jesus said, "Do not store up for yourselves treasures on earth, where moth and rust destroy, and where thieves break in and steal" (Matt. 6:19). The apostle John puts it this way: "Do not work for food that spoils, but for food that endures to eternal life" (John 6:27). There are things worth working for in this life. An excessity isn't one of them.

Steve discovered that pornography is food that spoils. Ultimately, so is any *Gotta Have It!* behavior. It cannot deliver on its promises.

It's amazing how much spoilage people are willing to endure in order to continue with their excessities. There were times in Steve's journey to recovery where he returned to pornography, even after working to realize its spoiled nature. It's that way so often with different addictions. It reminds me of 2 Peter 2:22: "Of them the proverbs are true: 'A dog returns to its vomit,' and, 'A sow that is washed goes back to her wallowing in the mud.'" Excessities don't want you to see the spoilage, the vomit, the mud they really are, so they lie. If you have to endure in this life, why would you want to endure for spoilage, vomit, and mud? Why not choose to endure for something better, something that lasts?

BLESSED ENDURANCE

Scripture says that God's love endures forever (1 Chron. 16:34; Ps. 136), His righteousness endures forever (Ps. 111:3), His faithfulness endures forever (Ps. 117:2), His laws endure forever (Ps. 119:91), His name endures forever (Ps. 135:13), and His sovereignty endures forever (Lam. 5:19). God is an enduring God.

God is the epitome of endurance. He constantly has to undergo the consequences of our behavior, yet He does not give in; He continues to act within His loving nature even where we are concerned. We are reminded of this in Acts 13:17–19, which says, "The God of the people of Israel chose our fathers; he made the people prosper during their stay in Egypt, with mighty power he led them out of that country, he endured their conduct for about forty years in the desert, he overthrew seven nations in Canaan and gave their land to his people as their inheritance." I love the middle part of this passage where it says that God "endured" their conduct. As comfortable as it would be for me to relegate that type of "conduct" to the people of Israel thousands of years ago, I know that God endures my conduct today. Just as He continued to bless the people of Israel, despite their conduct, He does the same thing to me.

God endures my conduct and loves and blesses me anyway because He embodies the second part of the definition of endurance, which is to accept or tolerate even something irritating. I can be very irritating to God, but He endures with me because He loves me.

Endurance also has the connotation of existing in the same state without changing. This is truly a definition of God. Numbers 23:19 says, "God is not a man, that he should lie, nor a son of man, that he should change his mind. Does he speak and then not act? Does he promise and not fulfill?" God is who He is, period. Hebrews 13:8 puts it pretty succinctly: "Jesus Christ is the same yesterday and today and forever."

We need only look to Jesus to see the embodiment of the final definition of endurance, which is to remain firm under suffering or misfortune without yielding: "Let us fix our eyes on Jesus, the author and perfecter of our faith, who for the joy set before him endured the cross, scorning its shame, and sat down at the right hand of the throne of God. Consider him who endured such opposition from sinful men, so that you will not grow weary and lose heart" (Heb. 12:2–3). Jesus endured so we can endure, so we will not grow weary and lose heart.

Endurance, like patience, is a gift from God. God has it and wants to give it to you. Romans 15:5 says that God gives endurance and encouragement. The verse just before that says, "Everything that was written in the past was written to teach us, so that through endurance and the encouragement of the Scriptures we might have hope" (15:4).

So, how are you doing in the endurance department? How are you living out the definition of *endurance* in your own life? Is your endurance being used to engage in your excessities, or is it being used to help you refrain from them? If you want God to give you endurance, you need to make sure you're going to put His gift to the right use.

Planting Seeds

I have seen people endure quite a lot for the sake of their excessity. I've seen alcoholics endure the steady poisoning of their bodies until they are so physically dependent upon alcohol, stopping would be life threatening. I've seen gamblers endure the humiliation of lying again and again to family members and friends to get money. I've seen women endure prostitution for drugs. I've seen people endure the slow strangulation of their significant relationships in exchange for an excessity. I've seen people endure physical deterioration and significant health issues because of saying yes over and over again.

What are you enduring in order to hold on to your excessity? What have you decided to put up with in order to continue to engage in your *Gotta Have It!* behavior? Earlier in the book, you did some similar exercises, but you're far enough in now that you've probably been making some small, positive changes. However, certain excessities or *Gotta Have It!* behaviors may be proving harder to tackle than others. Those are the ones I want to address in the questions above. I want you to be honest and start looking at the real-life consequences of choosing to continue with your excessity.

What I endure for my excessity:

1.

2.

3.

4.

5.

Getting over an excessity will require all the endurance you've developed up to this point and then some. It will require you to stay very close to God and to use His voice to counter the deceptions of the excessity. And it will require this commitment over and over and over again. Your *Gotta Have It!* behavior has established a pattern in your life. In order to overcome, you will need to stand against the tide of desire, fear, anger, pleasure, or stubbornness that your excessity sends against you.

Here is the continuum that Steve endured. As you read over the steps, I want you to be honest and circle where you are right now:

1. I think I can outrun the negative consequences of my excessity.

2. My excessity is intruding unwanted into other areas of my life.

3. I realize how out of balance my life has become because of my excessity.

4. Because of my excessity, my relationships are damaged and suffer from lack of trust.

5. I am willing to risk exposure in order to gain control over my excessity.

6. I am willing to become vulnerable to others in order to gain help over my excessity.

7. I am willing to endure the consequences so I can overcome my excessity and refuse any longer to yield to it.

Engaging in each excessity represents a loss in your life. Maybe it's the respect of your family. Maybe it's the trust of a spouse. Maybe it's your physical health. Maybe it's the affection of your children. Maybe it's your own relationship with God. You've given up something in order to sustain your excessity. At this moment, you are enduring the results of those losses.

God has bigger and better things for you to use your endurance for. Do not expect Him to give you endurance in order to continue with your alcoholism or your gambling or your workaholism or your spending or your food frenzies. Why would He give you endurance to run headlong into further damage or even death? The endurance He wants to give you is for eternal purposes. Give Him your trust by setting down your excessities, and watch what blessings He pours into your hands: "Give, and it will be given to you. A good measure, pressed down, shaken together and running over, will be poured into your lap. For with the measure you use, it will be measured to you" (Luke 6:38). If you give up your excessities to God, be prepared; the blessings you receive will overflow in your life.

Dear Father, I am ashamed of the things I have endured in order to go my own way, in order to keep doing what I want to do instead of doing what I know I should. I need to turn my endurance around and use it instead to endure for Your sake and for the sake of Your will in my life. I confess I need to learn to trust You more. Help me see clearly the consequences of my behaviors. Give me courage to change and the strength to endure the battle for change in my life. In this race called life, help me run to You with endurance.

10

God Provides Contentment

*I am not saying this because I am in need, for
I have learned to be content whatever the
circumstances. I know what it is to be in need,
and I know what it is to have plenty. I have
learned the secret of being content in any and
every situation, whether well fed or hungry,
whether living in plenty or in want. (Phil. 4:11–12)*

Happiness, satisfaction, and *fulfillment* are all words that are synonymous with contentment. Excessities promise to provide it. Yet excessities are firmly rooted in the *if-then.* They promise that *if* you give in to them, *then* you'll be happy, satisfied, or fulfilled in some way. I think we've begun to see how hollow that promise can be.

Real contentment, by contrast, isn't conditional. The apostle Paul had contentment; it was real and operating in his life, as evidenced in his letter to the Philippians. His contentment wasn't an *if-then* thing; it was an *always* thing. He wasn't waiting for certain conditions to be just right in order to be content. On the contrary—his contentment was a present reality, regardless of circumstance.

Excessities and contentment are like fire and water. If water is stronger, it puts out fire, but if fire is stronger, it consumes water. Fire and water are in competition with each other. Excessities are in competition with contentment. If you're content, excessities lose their force in your life. In order to gain the upper hand, excessities compel you to concentrate on what you want instead of to realize what you have.

NEVER ENOUGH

Remember the "never enough" activities that we talked about in chapter 2—those secret activities or behaviors that we just can't seem to get enough of? It is not possible to realize and experience true contentment if you are focused on "never enoughs." We need to discover what they are and move them out of the way so contentment can flow into our lives.

The Bible is filled with examples of "never enough" behaviors. We'll just look at one example right now, from Isaiah: "They are dogs with mighty appetites; they never have enough. They are shepherds who lack understanding; they all turn to their own way, each seeks his own gain" (56:11).

This passage is directed to the elders of Israel who turned aside from how they were supposed to act—as protectors, leaders, and guides to their flock—and went off on their own way, seeking their own gain. This is a textbook example of how excessities get turned around into "never enoughs." Often the behavior of an excessity starts out as harmless, even beneficial. Hobbies, for example, can be recreational and completely appropriate. Pursuing your career can be productive and positive. Eating and drinking in moderation are beneficial. Relationships can be giving and loving. At some point, however, each of these activities can turn and turn out a different way. A hobby becomes an all-consuming obsession. Working becomes workaholism. Eating becomes gluttony. Drinking becomes drunkenness. Relationships become twisted. When you start down this road without a proper understanding of the dangers, they can end up turning on you, spiraling back down into themselves. At some point the behavior becomes an excessity. When it does, you no longer have control over it.

THE GOSPEL ACCORDING TO DOROTHY

I grew up watching the movie *The Wizard of Oz*. I especially liked it as a kid because I lived in Kansas. The movie would play almost every holiday, usually when kids were home from school on break and parents needed a few extra hours to finish up with holiday preparations. I watched it so many times I could run the dialogue. Even as a kid, there was one part near the end that always drew my attention, though I didn't really understand it at the time. Dorothy has just returned from Oz, and she's telling her uncle's hired hands what she's learned during her journey. Dorothy says she's learned that "if I ever go looking for my heart's desire again, I won't look any further than my own backyard; because if it isn't there, I never really lost it to begin with."

The gospel according to Dorothy tells me that contentment isn't something external, found in circumstances or even adventures. Contentment is an internal condition, something you shouldn't need to look for because its rightful home is in your heart. Dorothy learned to recognize the value of what she had instead of seeking after the promise of what she didn't.

The ability to capture true contentment comes from recognizing what you have instead of focusing on what you don't. The writer of Hebrews put it this way: "Keep your lives free from the love of money and be content with what you have, because God has said, 'Never will I leave you; never will I forsake you'" (13:5). Removing "the love of money" in this passage, each one of us could substitute our own particular desire that fuels our excessity. "Keep[ing] [our] lives free" would be difficult to do if it weren't for the "because" statement that follows. Why can you put down your desire, your longing, your need, your excessity? Because by saying no to it, you are saying yes to God, knowing that through His love He has promised never to leave you, never to forsake you.

Planting Seeds

In *The Wizard of Oz*, Dorothy runs away from home rather than face the problems brewing over her beloved dog, Toto. Excessities are often ways to run away. Food, alcohol, work, games, hobbies, and relationships are all ways people use to run away from their problems or the discomfort they experience because of their problems. In this Planting Seeds section, I'd like you to specifically identify the ways you still "run away from home"—"home" being your life. These are your entrenched behaviors. Even after all you've read, you may still eat too much, watch too much television, shop too much, or talk too much. You may still become incensed and angry too often, or bury yourself in your job, or isolate yourself too much from others. Write down what it is you still do. Take time, and mentally go through all aspects of your day. Take note of the first things that come to mind, but don't just stop there. Be still, and think about what you do each and every day.

I still run away from home when I …

1.

2.

3.

4.

5.

6.

7.

When Dorothy ran away from home, she did so for a reason: a nasty neighbor, Miss Gulch, had threatened to destroy Dorothy's dog, Toto, for getting into her yard. Similarly, when you "run away from home," you have reasons. For each of the ways you still run away from home, I want you to write down the reason. At this point, you should have a pretty good idea what each of those reasons are. What are you still trying to escape by running in this way?

I am still escaping …

1.

2.

3.

4.

5.

6.

7.

At the end of the movie, Dorothy realizes she was running away trying to find something she should have had all along. She thought about all of the blessings of being home and utters the famous refrain "There's no place like home." In this instance, "home" is you, who you are right now. For at least as many reasons as you stated for running away, I'd like you now to state blessings or benefits for staying home, for being you, right now. There is no place like home, and there is no one else like you. Think about the progress you've made and how far you've come on some of your *Gotta Have It!* behaviors. Use this as a way to celebrate your progress. Working through your excessities is a process, and part of that process is taking stock, every now and again, in order to recognize how far you've come.

Ways I am blessed:

1.

2.

3.

4.

5.

6.

7.

For some of you, that last exercise was difficult because you are not comfortable or familiar with considering yourself blessed. If that was difficult for you, I'd like you to consider shifting your focus from you as the blessed to God as the One who blesses. Try the exercise again, this time thinking about God and the ways He has blessed your life. Concentrate not on the material things God has given you but on the more intangible gifts, the gifts that stretch through time and persevere regardless of circumstances. God is not a cosmic Santa; He is a sovereign and holy God. His gifts are not the equivalent of party favors, meant to delight for the moment. Think below the surface, into the deeper realms of God's blessings in your life.

This week, you've got an extra-credit assignment. I'd like you to watch *The Wizard of Oz*. Watch it in light of what the characters each learn along the way, about themselves, about contentment, about finding their hearts' desires. Just be sure to watch the Judy Garland version and not one of the newer, cartoon-type versions.

Make God the center and focus of your life. Set Him squarely in the middle, and allow Him to topple all the other pretenders and idols you've erected through your excessities and *Gotta Have It!* behaviors. Ask Him to teach you how to fear Him with love and trust. Ask Him to teach you, like Paul, the secret to contentment. Then be ready to give up what you don't need so you can grasp onto what you do.

> Lord, I praise You for Your mercy, love,
> and grace to me. I thank You for the
> blessings You've poured into my life.

Help me be able to see each and every one more clearly. Help me see You more clearly. I confess I have sought contentment down wrong roads and paths that led me further from You. Teach me to see clearly so I can follow the paths of righteousness that lead to You. Help me fear You more than I fear my excessities so that I may have life, a life of contentment no matter what circumstances it holds for me.

11

God Provides Wisdom

In the house of the wise are stores of
choice food and oil, but a foolish man
devours all he has. (Prov. 21:20)

Wise people are deliberate and thoughtful. They take circumstances into account. Wise people know when to stop. Foolish people have no "off switch." Once activated, they just keep going, as the verse above says, devouring all they have. They live lives overrun by excessity. No one wants to be considered foolish, but if we are honest that's exactly how we could categorize our *Gotta Have It!* behaviors.

BRAD'S STORY

This verse makes me think of someone I'll call Brad, a successful businessman. You might even say a wise businessman, since his professional acumen was sought after and highly prized in his community. After creating several lucrative companies, Brad was on the A-list for social functions, speaking engagements, and civic events. As his notoriety spread, he began to travel more away from home. This put added pressure on his time in town as he continued to keep a handle on his businesses. Certainly, he had people running various aspects of them, but, being a wise businessman, Brad also knew the importance of "hands on" in managing and maintaining what he had. He knew no one else would take care of his businesses the way he could.

To the business and social world around him, Brad was a wise man. However, there was an aspect of Brad's life that failed to exhibit the same measure of wisdom. In this part of his life, Brad was markedly unwise. Brad, in his headlong rush to achieve, maintain, and increase his commercial success, was a fool at home. With all of his time and energies diverted into business, he was devouring the stores of natural affection and goodwill of his family. He failed to discern the inner qualities of his children because he was rarely home and seldom spent any meaningful time with them. He failed to recognize the value of his relationship with his wife because he so consistently took it for granted.

Brad told himself that all of his hard work was providing and securing a future for his family. He thought his wife would appreciate his sacrifice and understand the time away as a necessary "evil." Brad didn't understand that what he was really securing was a future without his children, as they painfully disengaged from his life and found substitutes—though sometimes very poor ones—for his presence. Brad didn't understand when his wife began to think of his time away not as a necessary "evil" but as just plain evil, when she came to view his work as his mistress. For all of his understanding of the need to be hands on at work, Brad failed to understand the need to be hands on at home. When it came to his family, Brad was a fool to jeopardize something so valuable for monetary and social success.

WISDOM 101

An excess, by its very nature, is generally an unwise thing. For us, excess means more than necessary. Excess is what gets us in trouble. Again, a person needs to work but shouldn't become a workaholic. A person needs clothing but shouldn't become a shopaholic. A person needs to eat but shouldn't become a glutton. A glass of wine is fine unless you're an alcoholic. A simple wager has no harm unless you're a pathological gambler. A hobby isn't a hobby if it's your one true satisfaction in life. Excessities blur the line between something that is fine and something that is over the line. When we're caught in the spiral of an excessity, we can find it very difficult to judge where that line is and how and when to draw ourselves back from the edge. We need Wisdom 101.

I've never seen Wisdom 101 in any college course listing. While institutions of higher learning are the world's answer to knowledge, there are fortunately other sources available for attaining wisdom. In Scripture, Wisdom 101 is called the book of Proverbs. It was written by King Solomon, the wisest man who ever lived. Here is its course description: "The proverbs of Solomon son of David, king of Israel: for attaining wisdom and discipline; for understanding words of insight; for acquiring a disciplined and prudent life, doing what is right and just and fair" (Prov. 1:1–3). This book is an amazingly practical and sometimes amusing treatise on the benefits of wisdom and the pitfalls of foolishness. Verse after verse and example after example juxtapose the behavior and the consequences of the wise and the fool, the prudent and the simple.

A proverb is a fundamental truth—a short saying that describes the way things actually are. For this reason, proverbs are the perfect foil for excessities, which operate on deception rather than truth and distort the ways things actually are. As we've talked about before, the distortion and the deception of excessities are designed to keep you chained to them; proverbs, therefore, can assist in uncovering truth and dissipating the power of excessities.

There are a vast number of things we can learn from Proverbs, and a thorough, thoughtful reading of it is tremendously beneficial as a first step to attaining wisdom. There are thirty-one chapters—one for every day of any month. Here are just a few proverbs I pulled out from the "course." These are merely provided to, hopefully, whet your appetite to investigate this Wisdom 101, the book of Proverbs, further:

> The prudent see danger and take refuge,
> but the simple keep going and suffer for it.
> (Prov. 27:12).

The last thing an excessity wants you to do is slow down, stop, think it over, and evaluate the evidence. Excessities urge you to just keep going, keep doing what you're doing, regardless of the results and evidence to the contrary.

> I, wisdom, dwell with prudence; I possess
> knowledge and discretion. (Prov. 8:12)

In this verse, knowledge is seen as an addition to wisdom, not a substitute for it. Knowledge is a component of wisdom, but knowledge is not a guarantee of wisdom. Knowledge, without wisdom, is just a recitation of facts. Wisdom allows the knowledge to be placed into context and utilized to its full potential. Lastly, wisdom is coupled with discretion. Discretion is the ability to accurately read the choices you are presented with and make the correct decision. Because of this, it's no wonder discretion is a companion of wisdom! How in the world could you accomplish something as tricky as discretion without wisdom? Wisdom, then, is a conglomeration of several words and abilities, all pointing to a capability to understand the way things really are and act accordingly.

> Fools are headstrong and do what they like;
> wise people take advice. (Prov. 12:15 MSG)

I used *The Message* translation here because I liked its succinct wording. You could very easily take out the word *fools* and put in the word *excessities*. Excessities don't want you to get advice. They just want you to keep doing what you're doing. Wise people, however, develop a built-in *wait-a-minute* feature that is able to step on the brakes and seek out the counsel of others, listening to something other than the urgency of the excessity. Wise people take advice and, being wise, they make sure they're asking someone wiser. Wise people are also humble people who are able to recognize when they need outside help and actively seek out and accept that help.

> He who gets wisdom loves his own soul;
> he who cherishes understanding prospers. (Prov.
> 19:8)

Wisdom is about feeding your inner part, your soul. Excessities are about satisfying the outer, surface parts. Wisdom is about making a choice to deny the outer in order to truly nourish the inner. When you are able to make this difficult choice and feed your soul instead of your excessity, you will prosper. This is a promise, a true promise—not the false, deceptive promises made by any one of your *Gotta Have It!* behaviors.

WISDOM'S PLAN OF ACTION

Solomon didn't write a book full of flowery platitudes and wouldn't-it-be-nice-if statements. Instead, it is a very practical book, full of situations and circumstances with present-day, right-now applications. One of those applications is found in Proverbs 2:1–11, where Solomon provides a series of action steps for the reader to take to begin to incorporate wisdom into his or her life. I believe these steps are applicable to gaining wisdom and overcoming an excessity:

> My son, if you accept my words
>   and store up my commands within you,
> turning your ear to wisdom
>   and applying your heart to understanding,
> and if you call out for insight
>   and cry aloud for understanding,

and if you look for it as for silver
    and search for it as for hidden treasure,
then you will understand the fear of the LORD
    and find the knowledge of God.
For the LORD gives wisdom,
    and from his mouth come knowledge and
    understanding.
He holds victory in store for the upright,
    he is a shield to those whose walk is blameless,
for he guards the course of the just
    and protects the way of his faithful ones.
Then you will understand what is right and just
    and fair—every good path.
For wisdom will enter your heart,
    and knowledge will be pleasant to your soul.
Discretion will protect you,
    and understanding will guard you.

I think it would be good to take this passage apart and look at each component separately.

Step 1: Accept the Truth and Store Up God's Word

My son, if you accept my words
    and store up my commands within you

In order to incorporate wisdom, you have to accept the truth of any given situation, thought, or feeling. Often, I've found that people really do know the truth. The problem comes in accepting that truth into their lives because of the pain, disappointment, fear, or other negatives they associate with the truth. Truth may *represent* something negative, but truth is not negative in and of itself. God is called the God of truth. Psalm 31:5 says, "Into your hands I commit my spirit; redeem me, O LORD, the God of truth." Jesus Himself spoke these words at the point of His death on the cross. God is able to redeem the truth. He did it for Jesus, and He is able to do it for you. An excessity does not want you to accept the truth, and it certainly doesn't want that truth redeemed. A redeemed truth deflates the power of the excessity.

Fighting the temptation of excessities is draining. It is important, therefore, to store up reserves in order to maintain your commitment to live wisely, apart from out-of-control *Gotta Have It!* behaviors. God's Word is God's truth. You'll need this to counter the lies of the excessity. Store it up; take in as much as you can, so you'll have it when you need it.

Step 2: Be Careful What You Listen to and Apply

turning your ear to wisdom
and applying your heart to understanding

Be sure to keep your ears tuned in to what wisdom is telling you. Refuse to listen any longer to the murmurs of your excessity. Refute the lies you hear with the truth you've learned through the wisdom you've gained. Renounce the lies for what they are.

It takes effort to continue participating in an excessity. The toll on your whole person—emotions, relationships, body, spirit—is taxing, often more so the longer you participate. Excessities require application. Solomon says here to use that energy, that application for a better purpose. He wants you to apply your heart to understanding. Applying your heart to an excessity just breeds more need to continue the excessity. Applying your heart to understanding produces strength, courage, and perseverance to resist the pull of the excessity.

Step 3: Ask for Help

> and if you call out for insight
> and cry aloud for understanding

When seeking after wisdom, there are times you will need to ask for help from others. I believe there is great power in confessing your need for wisdom and in asking others to help you find it. You widen the circle of your defenses and gather the strength and wisdom of others to your aid.

Besides other people, you have another source for help. Remember Philippians 4:6–7? "Do not be anxious about anything, but in everything, by prayer and petition, with thanksgiving, present your requests to God. And the peace of God, which transcends all understanding, will guard your hearts and your minds in Christ Jesus." Cry aloud to God for understanding and don't feel self-conscious about it. James 1:5 says, "If any of you lacks wisdom, he should ask God, who gives generously to all without finding fault, and it will be given to him." Ask and you will receive. Keep asking.

Step 4: Keep Your Eyes Open and Believe

> and if you look for it as for silver
> and search for it as for hidden treasure,
>
> then you will understand the fear of the LORD
> and find the knowledge of God.

Wisdom is not always something easily seen. It takes a discerning and watchful eye. There are lessons to be learned and wisdom to be gained in unlikely places, sometimes hidden from view. It will require you to do some personal digging around in your life and excessities.

It can be very disheartening to continue to look for something you don't believe you'll ever find. Most of the time, you'll probably just give up and figure the effort and energy aren't worth it. Excessities whisper unbelief, so you will need to constantly revisit step 3. God promises that you will understand and find.

Step 5: Consider the Source

> For the LORD gives wisdom,
> and from his mouth come knowledge and
> understanding.

God is the source of wisdom, knowledge, and understanding. These are not things you must generate completely on your own. Instead of concentrating on your own ability to gain wisdom, choose to focus on God's ability to give it to you. Remember, with God all things are possible—even making you a wise person.

Step 6: Trust God to Protect You

> He holds victory in store for the upright,
> > he is a shield to those whose walk is blameless,
>
> for he guards the course of the just
> > and protects the way of his faithful ones.

When you submit yourself to God, you join His team. This is a smart move because God's team wins; God holds victory in store for His team. In the meantime, He acts as your shield. He guards you and protects your way. When God is placed in this position in your life—as shield, guardian, and protector—you will have no need for the false security of an excessity. Nothing an excessity promises will compare.

Step 7: Know There Is a Light at the End of the Tunnel

> Then you will understand what is right and just
> > and fair—every good path.

When you're in the thick of battle, it can be hard to see beyond the present struggle to the victory ahead. That's why this verse is so important. It is a promise that you will understand what is right and just and fair. Stumbling around in the dark and twisted path of an excessity is not what God has in mind for your future! You will know and be able to see every good path for your life.

Step 8: Claim the Prize

> For wisdom will enter your heart,
> and knowledge will be pleasant to your soul.
>
> Discretion will protect you,
> and understanding will guard you.

There is a prize that awaits this search for wisdom. The prize is wisdom itself, along with knowledge, discretion, and understanding. God is not in the carrot-dangling business. There is a finish line to wisdom He means for you to cross, even if He has to carry you over it Himself.

Planting Seeds

For this Planting Seeds section, I'd like you to think about shifting—the shifting sand of excessities and shifting your foundations for life over from your excessities to something much firmer, much wiser. Jesus begins the story of the wise man, found in Matthew 7:24–27, by saying, "Therefore everyone who hears these words of mine and puts them into practice is like a wise man who built his house on the rock" (v. 24). I'd like you to think about how you can obtain wisdom and become a rock dweller.

To begin with, ask yourself the following questions:

Who do you know or who have you known in your life that you count as a wise person?

How did that person demonstrate wisdom?

Have you ever asked that person how his or her wisdom was acquired? If so, what were you told?

Have you ever asked that person for his or her advice? If so, what was the advice?

If you were given advice, did you follow it? If so, what was the outcome?

Do you think you are a wise person about some aspects of your life? If so, what are those aspects?

Do you think you are an unwise person about some aspects of your life? If so, what are those aspects?

Are you willing to ask God for wisdom? If yes, do you really believe He will give it to you?

That last answer is very important. Earlier, you read the James 1:5 passage that says God generously gives wisdom to all who ask Him. There is, however, a disclaimer on that promise that comes in verse 6: "But when he asks, he must believe and not doubt, because he who doubts is like a wave on the sea, blown and tossed by the wind." Attaining wisdom requires faith. You must believe. Hebrews 11:6 says, "And without faith it is impossible to please God, because anyone who comes to him must believe that he exists and that he rewards those who earnestly seek him."

I recognize that some of you may be feeling disheartened reading that because you believe you do not have the necessary faith. I would argue that your life with your excessities shows a great amount of faith. You have just placed your capacity for faith in the wrong things. Instead of building your faith on the sand of excessities, shift that faith over to the bedrock of God. Your life with your excessities has demonstrated a tenacious capacity for faith, for belief, with very little to show for it. How much greater will your faith be and grow when you place it in something—in Someone—trustworthy and powerful and worthy of your faith and belief? Excessities are idols, false gods people use to feel better about themselves, to provide meaning, comfort, and security. For millennia, God has been in the business of toppling those idols and calling people to worship Him instead.

Therefore, I urge you to bring whatever level of faith you have to God and allow Him to fortify it, to expand it, to validate it in your own life. Start with Solomon's step 1—accept the truth of God and begin to store up God's Word in your heart. Read over the book of Proverbs; study one chapter a day for the next thirty-one days. Apply what you learn, take it to heart, and force out the excessities residing there. Ask God for wisdom, and believe that when it says He gives to *all*, what it really means is He gives to *you*.

> God of truth and wisdom, fill my heart.
> Crowd out the doubt and unbelief that

fester there. Help me truly know and accept that You are able to give me the wisdom to change. When I doubt myself, fortify my trust in You. When I become weak, remind me of Your strength. Drown out all of the other voices so that I will hear Your voice of encouragement alone. Increase my faith to know You are able to give me wisdom and discernment to face each day and each temptation.

12

God Provides Hope

*A horse is a vain hope for deliverance; despite
all its great strength it cannot save. (Ps. 33:17)*

Every time you reach for one of your excessities, you saddle up a horse of hope. You mount up and ride off toward deliverance. You think that horse of hope is going to help you outrun whatever it is that fuels your excessities, whether it's loneliness, fear, guilt, anger, discomfort, or anxiety. You hop into the saddle and hope maybe this time it will work. The more often you saddle up, the stronger that excessity becomes in your life, but as the verse above says, *despite all its strength it cannot save.*

Excessities gain their strength, their hope, from you; you infuse the excessity with hope. Your hopes are only as strong as you are, and the more strength you pour into your excessity, the weaker you become. Just as you can run a horse into the ground, your excessities can run your hope into the ground.

KEVIN'S STORY
Kevin was exhausted. It was a struggle just to get up and function

every day. Sleep was elusive and often seemed more trouble than it was worth. He'd wake up in the morning—whatever the hour—apprehensive and anxious for the day ahead. The weight of work responsibilities and the financial realities of his current situation chained him to a sort of emotional and physical lethargy. Kevin felt like all eyes were watching him—his wife, his kids, even his employees seemed to be watching to see what he was going to do and how he was going to make things better. Yet the weight of trying to make things bearable had become unbearable to Kevin. Life was heavy and hope harder and harder to find.

At first, his secretive forays down the interstate to the casino were sporadic, but Kevin soon found he only felt invigorated and *alive* during these times. Even when he lost money, he still felt the pull of an anticipated win. Afterward, though, on too many drives home, the guilt descended. It just didn't seem right, somehow, that the only time he felt energized and relieved should be doing something he knew was wrong. Slowly, Kevin began to equate that weight of guilt with the rest of the burdens he felt, the burdens he resented and had turned to gambling to forget. Kevin began to see his time at the casino as necessary, as a coping mechanism, and, frankly, as the true highlight of his week.

Kevin found himself heading off to gamble more often during the week, sometimes even during the workday. He kept hoping that it would get him through this rough patch in his life and that as soon as things calmed down he wouldn't need to do it as much. He kept hoping … right up until the day it all crashed around him and he found himself in danger of financial ruin and losing his family.

THE POWER OF HOPE

To understand the true power of hope, I think it's a good idea to contemplate what the world would look like without hope. It is a world without anticipation, without desire or expectation—a flat, monochrome world with only a single *what-is* view. First Chronicles 29:15 calls it a shadow world.

Over my time in counseling, I have seen too many people trapped in this shadow world without true hope. I have seen them desperately reach for anything—harmful, dangerous, destructive, false—to try to provide some sort of color of hope in the shadow. Imagine my position—within their world without hope I have to tell them that the one thing they cling to for a modicum of hope really isn't hope at all. I have to point out the painfully obvious: The hope they cling to—whatever it is—is false hope.

If this is all I did and all I could offer, I wouldn't do it. It would be too bleak. I praise God, however, that my job isn't just to point out false hope but to point toward *true* hope. This is hope that sings with a symphony of desire, expectation, trust, sweet anticipation, and even sweeter fulfillment. This is hope that sings with God's voice. This is not a shadow world; it is quite literally heaven. And what I get to do is show people the way to find their own patch of heaven on earth, through an understanding and connection to true hope.

Now that's a job I believe in. It's why The Center I founded twenty-five years ago has become known as *a place of hope*. It is a place where people find the strength and courage to give up their false hopes and the joy to discover their true hope. Hope has come to color everything we do, from the name of our Web site to titles on my books to our theme verse of Jeremiah 29:11. People come to us riding on the exhausted, failing horses of false hope and leave soaring on the wings of true hope.

LEAP OF FAITH

This is not an easy journey. It's not even an intuitive one for many. Letting go of the reins of a false hope in order to place yourself within reach of true hope is very much a leap of faith.

I love the Indiana Jones movies with Harrison Ford. There is a scene in the third movie, *Indiana Jones and the Last Crusade,* where in order to save his dying father, Indy must successfully navigate a series of tests to reach the Holy Grail. At one point, Indy reaches a place where he must make a proverbial leap of faith. Finding himself thwarted on the wrong side of a bottomless chasm, Indy must leap out into the apparent nothingness of space in order to keep going. He steels himself and steps out into the air of the abyss, only to land on a thin stone bridge that was impossible to see before. Once he realizes the path is there, that it is real, he successfully makes his way safely across to find the Grail and save his father. The path across was there the whole time; he just couldn't see it. The only way to see it was to trust it was there.

The leap between false hope and true hope can be very much like that step into nothingness. On the one side, the false hope seems so substantial, so present, so *there.* The false hope is a known quantity. Even though a part of you knows it doesn't live up to its promises, even though a part of you knows you won't get to where you need to go by sticking to your false hope, another part of you is terrified of the abyss you're stepping out into in order to grasp hold of true hope.

You are terrified of the unseen. It is that unseen nature of true hope that requires this leap of faith. Romans 8:24 reminds us about this unseen nature when it says, "But hope that is seen is no hope at all. Who hopes for what he already has?"

With an excessity, you know what you already have. Hopefully, by now, you recognize that what you have really isn't much and that you've been putting all of your hope and trust in a dead horse, unable to save you. It's time to let go of the known—the seen—and reach toward something better, something unseen. It's time to take your own leap of faith where hope is concerned. To quote from the Shakespearean play *Hamlet,* "There are more things in heaven and earth than are dreamt of in your philosophy."[1] Just because you can't see something doesn't mean it isn't there.

Hope, then, is a leap of faith. Hope and faith are linked. It takes faith to hope, and hope fuels faith. Hebrews 11:1 says, "Now faith is being sure of what we hope for and certain of what we do not see." Up to this point, you have put a certain measure of faith and hope into your excessity. Against evidence to the contrary, you've continued to get on that horse and ride toward a deliverance that never materializes. Keep the hope and faith, but ditch the excessity. It's time to place your hope and faith in something more reliable, more trustworthy, than an excessity.

A PLACE OF HOPE

In this life, there is nothing outside of God that is reliable, permanent, and unchanging. When you anchor your hope to things tied up with this life, you will be disappointed. If you want to find hope fulfilled, you must place your hope in God. When you do this, your hope is safe; your hope is *true.* Hebrews 6:19 says that this hope is an anchor for your soul.

Here are just a few promises about putting your hope in God. I venture to say that all of the other things you've been pinning your hopes on are unable to claim the same:

> God promises in Psalm 25:3 that if you hope in Him, you will never be put to shame for that hope. How many times have you been ashamed of where else you've placed your hope?

> God promises in Psalm 31:24 strength and courage for all those who hope in Him. How many times have your strength and courage failed you because of where you've placed your hope?

> God promises in Psalm 33:18 to watch over you and love you when you place your hope in Him. In all of the things you've put your hope in, which one of them has ever had the capacity to protect and love you?

> God promises in Psalm 62:5 to give rest to those who hope in Him. Further, He promises to be enough, to be sufficient, for the hope that is in you. Of all of the things you've put your hope in, which one ever gave you a true sense of rest and peace?

Which one proved to be enough, to be sufficient? Instead, didn't each one keep demanding more and more and more?

God promises in Isaiah 40:31 to renew your strength. Which of your excessities ever provided long-term renewal?

A TIME FOR HOPE

In the interest of full disclosure, I need to mention something here. It is how God differs from your excessities. You've already seen that God actually delivers hope, while excessities provide only a shadow. You've already seen that God is real, while the idols of excessity are hollow substitutions. Excessities, though they can take control, are still ultimately under your control. You set the time, the place, the amount. You even set what the reward is. You establish the parameters for your own excessity. Truly, you give the excessity power. God, however, is sovereign unto Himself. Again, He is not a cosmic Santa Claus, waiting for your Christmas list. He is not a supernatural genie in a bottle, waiting for you to rub the outside so He can grant your three wishes. He is not a celestial vending machine waiting for you to put in your coin of worship, praise, or prayer in order to dispense whichever blessing you choose at any given moment. It doesn't work that way. You're not dealing with a chunk of metal or a block of wood; you're dealing with a sovereign God, a deity, a creative personality outside yourself. As such, He has His own ideas about things and His own timing of when things get done.

Excessities are useful because they are often immediate. Granted, their benefits fade over time and use, but they are a time-specific activity. That's one of their most potent selling points. They offer relief, companionship, gratification, satisfaction, release— right now. Truthfully, with God, sometimes you simply have to wait. He has His own timing for things. Often, His timing is not yours or mine.

His timing can seem perplexing and even arbitrary. If I understand, feel, and experience my need to be so immediate, I can be left to wonder, why doesn't God? Waiting on God has become easier over the years, as I've learned to trust Him. It's also become easier as I've experienced being a parent myself. Sometimes my boys want something right now. However, as a father, I recognize there are implications and consequences they are not aware of that influence my decision on whether or not to say yes at any given time.

I take comfort in Deuteronomy 7:22, which says, "The LORD your God will drive out those nations before you, little by little. You will not be allowed to eliminate them all at once, or the wild animals will multiply around you." Sometimes "little by little" is the way to proceed. In my line of work, we call it by several names— "process," "journey," "recovery." Over the years I've come to call it "baby steps." Little by little allows things to adjust to each new reality. Little by little does involve waiting, but it also very much involves growing, changing, adapting, accepting. When placed in this context, little by little—another way of saying *waiting*—has tremendous benefit.

When you wait on an excessity, there is no benefit. When you wait on God, however, you realize a host of benefits. Here are some of the benefits listed in the Psalms: When you wait on the Lord, you are heard (5:3); you are strengthened (27:14); you are helped and protected (33:20); you are answered (38:15); you are responded to (40:1). Waiting on the Lord is a time of rich blessing; waiting on an excessity is just that—waiting.

In our instantaneous, gotta-have-it-now culture, waiting is not easy. It can seem as if waiting for an answer from God is no answer or a "no" answer. It is a temptation, then, while waiting on God, to lose the very thing you're looking for—hope. It's important to realize that what sounds to you like "no" may be God saying, "Not yet" or "Not that, but this." We don't always get what we want from God; sometimes we get something even better. Romans 5:3–5 says, "Not only so, but we also rejoice in our sufferings, because we know that suffering produces perseverance; perseverance, character; and character, hope. And hope does not disappoint us, because God has poured out his love into our hearts by the Holy Spirit, whom he has given to us." If waiting seems like suffering, take heart! Even this, God can turn into a blessing and produce a harvest of hope.

While you wait on the Lord (and all of us will at some point in our lives), I'd like you to remember a couple of things, things that should give you hope to wait. God has marvelous plans for you. Again, the theme verse of The Center: "'For I know the plans I have for you,' declares the LORD, 'plans to prosper you and not to harm you, plans to give you hope and a future'" (Jer. 29:11). God has promised a plan and hope and future for you. It is secure within God. The only way for you to miss out on it is to chase after other things, like idols you've manufactured, and reject what God has planned. Anchor your hope firmly in God, and you will not be disappointed. Every promise given will be fulfilled, "a good measure, pressed down, shaken together and running over" (Luke 6:38).

PRISONERS OF HOPE

Before we go to the Planting Seeds section, I want to speak to those who have been wounded by hope. Maybe you have hoped desperately for something that didn't come. Maybe you hoped that God would provide something or remove something or enable something that didn't take place. You are wounded, and the easy promises of an excessity seem so much more compelling than a God you think has stopped caring about you. You have been battered and bruised by life and circumstances and feel abandoned by others and by God.

To you I would say that no matter what has happened, God is still your refuge. Don't give up on Him because what you so desperately wanted didn't happen. The loss of what you wanted does not mean a loss of His love. A "no" to your plea is not the same as "I don't love you." The hope for what you wanted to happen may have died, but your hope and faith in God's love don't need to die along with it. While God may have said no to what you asked for, He will never say no to you.

In the book of Lamentations, the prophet Jeremiah was told a very big "no" by God. No, God would not step back from the destruction coming to Jerusalem and Judah. After coming to grips with this reality, Jeremiah wrote: "So I say, 'My splendor is gone and all that I had hoped from the LORD.' I remember my affliction and my wandering, the bitterness and the gall. I well remember them, and my soul is downcast within me. Yet this I call to mind and therefore I have hope: Because of the LORD's great love we are not consumed, for his compassions never fail" (3:18–22). As with Jeremiah, your hope for something may be gone, but hope itself still lives on because of how much God loves you.

Listen to this God who loves you, your Father in heaven, who has always planned for your hope in Him to be fulfilled: "Return to your fortress, O prisoners of hope; even now I announce that I will restore twice as much to you" (Zech. 9:12). If you are a prisoner of hope because of some trauma, tragedy, disappointment, or defeat, return to God, your fortress. Your excessities cannot protect you from the pain. Only God can comfort you and restore your hope through His unfailing love.

Planting Seeds

In this section, you'll think about and examine the sources of hope in your life. Let's start first with what you hope for from your excessities. As you've engaged in them, you expected a payoff for doing them. Write down those hopes, those desires, those expectations, those anticipations.

What I hope for from my excessity:

1.

2.

3.

4.

5.

Next, I'd like you to honestly evaluate the payoff you've received. In other words, did you get what you hoped for? In some cases, depending upon what you hoped for, the answer may be yes, but often the answer will be no. Whichever it is, write either "yes" or "no" next to each hope you listed.

Now, I'd like you to think about your hopes in a little different way. I'd like you to detach your hopes from your excessities and think about what you hope for from life, in general.

What I hope for from life:

1.

2.

3.

4.

5.

Are your hopes from your excessity the same as what you hope for from life? For those that are the same, answer these follow-up questions:

Has your excessity really given you what you hoped for from life?

If your excessity had been able to deliver, why is what you hoped for still on your life list?

Evaluating things honestly, has your excessity helped or hindered achieving what you hoped for?

If the excessity has helped you achieve it, is there a way to continue to achieve it without the excessity?

If the excessity has hindered you from achieving it, why are you still engaged in the excessity?

For the answers that are different, answer these questions:

If the excessity is not helping you achieve what you hope
for in your life, why are you engaging in it?

What are some ways you could achieve what you hope
for in your life apart from the ineffective excessity?

Lastly, I'd like you to think about your hope in God. What do
you hope from God for yourself and for your life?
What I hope for from God—my God list:

1.

2.

3.

4.

5.

Looking at this list, are you honestly able to obtain any of
these things outside of God? If you are, does it really have a place
on your God list?

For the things that belong on your God list, I'd like you to put
down any scriptures you know that contain a promise about what
you've written down. As you do your own personal study, make

sure to look for additional verses or thoughts to confirm your list. Also be aware of any verses or thoughts that argue against something you have placed on your God list. For example, if one of the items on your God list is "to experience no troubles," well, you already know that's not going to be confirmed by Scripture. (Think back to what Jesus said in Matthew 6:34 about each day having enough trouble of its own.) You may find a need to modify your God list. Instead of wishing for no troubles, you might want to say instead, "Help through troubles." In that case, you could put down John 16:33 as a confirmation, where Jesus says, "In this world you will have trouble. But take heart! I have overcome the world."

You've been planting seeds throughout each chapter, but the seeds I want you to plant in this section are the seeds of hope. My prayer is that these seeds will grow and mature in you. At the moment, you may be thinking that even if you have any seeds of hope left in you they are small and inconsequential. That's okay. Jesus spoke about little, insignificant seeds in Mark 4:30–32 and Luke 17:6. He said that even though a mustard seed was the smallest of all of the seeds, if you just planted it and let it grow, it would turn into such a large plant that even birds could perch on its mature branches. He said faith even as small as a mustard seed could do incredible things. Your seed of hope may be as small as a mustard seed, but if you combine that little seed of hope with the water of faith, stand back and watch it grow!

With true hope in your life, you will be strengthened against the siren song of the false hope of excessities. When you are strengthened by true hope, you'll be able to withstand the storms of life that before sent you running to the rickety shelter of your *Gotta Have It!* behavior. Infused with true hope, you'll be able to patiently wait for the outcome you cannot see but nonetheless know is there. As with Indiana Jones, the only way to see it is to trust that it's there.

> *Father, I thank You for being the God of hope. As Romans 15:13 says, fill me with all joy and peace as I learn to trust in You more each day. Allow me to overflow with hope and beat back the shadow world of hopelessness I sometimes feel. Strengthen me by Your power. Help me put my hope in You even when I have to wait. And when Your answer is no, remind me over and over again how much You love me.*

13

God Provides Help

In the same way, the Spirit helps us
in our weakness. (Rom. 8:26)

In a way, help is both a blessing and a curse. There is a good-news, bad-news quality to help. The bad news comes when you find yourself in such a dire situation where you absolutely, desperately need help. You're in trouble, and your own efforts are not enough to save you. When help is what you get, that's very good news, indeed.

You are at the end of your rope, up a creek without a paddle, in over your head. Choose whatever colorful metaphor you want to use, but they all have something in common: Help is not always something you're willing to accept. If you're at the end of your rope, you have to drop that rope and grasp onto another one you're not holding. If you're up a creek without a paddle, once given a paddle, you actually have to start paddling, often against the current. If you're in over your head, you have to decide to come up for air. Help is needed, help is offered, but help also has to be accepted. Help is a three-step process:

1. RECOGNIZING HELP IS NEEDED

Denise had reached the threshold of step one; she knew she needed help. Her anger, scathing sarcasm, and bitter outlook were poisoning her life. The worse it got, the further family and friends retreated to the outskirts of her affection. The worse it got, the easier it was to reach for food to calm and relieve her agitation. Her relationships shrank and her weight ballooned. Things were totally out of control, and Denise realized she needed help.

This was not a conclusion Denise arrived at easily. Over the years, she had fought hard in her life not to need anything. She grew up to be in charge, in control, a self-sufficient person who was supposed to guide, direct, and delegate to others. Help was something Denise believed she was supposed to provide others. Help, she thought, was something strong people like her were obligated to provide to other—weaker—people. Help was something you responded with, not something you needed yourself.

During my first counseling session with Denise, she spent most of the time forcefully going over why she wasn't the sort of person who really needed help. It became immediately apparent that while Denise had reluctantly acceded to the possibility I might be of some small help to her, she was firmly in control of whether or not she accepted that help.

She reminded me of a house with a plethora of "No Trespassing," "No Soliciting," "Do Not Enter," and "Warning: Guard Dog on Duty" signs posted everywhere. Intrigued, I could only hope that Denise would trust me enough to allow me past her carefully con-structed barriers. Denise wanted help, but she only wanted it yelled across the safety of the sidewalk—not whispered from inside the locked chamber of her heart and emotions. I needed to get inside to be able to give her the help she really needed.

You're past step one by this time, aren't you? Haven't you come to accept that you need help controlling your urges, compulsions, addictions, patterns, behaviors—whatever way you've come to think of these debilitating, controlling excessities in your life? As they say, the first step to getting help is admitting you need it.

You're also on your way toward the second step, which is to find the right place to get help. There are plenty of places that offer help; that's often the problem. Many things are offered, but few are the real deal. Excessities feed off your need for help. They are parasitical, existing in a symbiotic relationship with your need. In this relationship, the excessity is the parasite (that which gains benefit), and you are the host (that which is used without true gain or benefit). Excessities aren't really interested in providing you with gain, benefit, or any real help for your need because without your need, they wouldn't have a place in your life. Excessities are great at keeping you firmly locked in step one, knowing you need help but going back to them again and again. They are not interested in letting you progress to step two, where you discover the right place to get help.

2. FINDING HELP

So where do you go to get the right help? Hopefully you're finding help in this book. Denise found help in my office. That's one of the places to find help—other people with something to share or help to offer. There needs to be an internal connection (trust) for this to work. Frankly, it can be quite a circuitous path to find the help you need.

I remember reading another book, *The Monster Within* by Cynthia McClure. Cynthia went to numerous people to try to find help for her bulimia back before most people knew what it was. There were people—professionals—who told her to "just stop it." There were people who told her what she really needed was a man in her life. There were people who just wanted to give her a pill to make the pain go away. Cynthia knew she needed help. She also knew the answers she was being given and the options offered weren't it. They didn't connect with her. It wasn't until she found someone willing to walk with her along the difficult road and inner journey to recovery that she found the help she needed.

Cynthia kept looking. She didn't give up because the first people she went to had no clue of how to help her. Determined, she kept searching and asking questions, evaluating the answers, and trying them on for size regarding her own issues. Eventually she found the right fit: someone who understood bulimia and who had an ability to understand Cynthia. When you can combine someone with the ability to really know who you are with the capacity to provide help, then you've arrived at help's step two with help, true help.

As a Christian, I believe that God is the ultimate source of true help. I believe that God has the ability to truly know who you are. I believe that God has the capacity to provide just the help you need. This question of where to find true help is age old. David asked and answered it himself in Psalm 121:1–2 when he said, "I lift up my eyes to the hills—where does my help come from? My help comes from the LORD, the Maker of heaven and earth." Psalm 46:1 reminds me that "God is our refuge and strength, an ever-present help in trouble."

Many of the people who come to The Center for help believe in God. Granted, some of them have had their faith severely shaken by the circumstances in their lives. Yet they cling to their belief and hope in a loving God, who is able to provide them with the help they need. They believe that God can work through us to provide them with a new direction for their lives and with a renewed understanding of all that is possible, including hope.

3. ACCEPTING HELP

Unlike so many of the false promises in this world, the help God gives is effective and tailored to our needs. The help He offers can also be different from what we asked for. Denise knew she needed help from me. The help she wanted was to have more control in her life. The help I offered was for her to have less. Denise thought the way out of her problems with the relationships in her life, including her relationship with food, was to attain an even greater level of self-control. Only a rigid stranglehold on her emotions and "weaknesses" was going to allow her to wrestle these problem areas to the ground so she could claim victory. She wanted weakness purged from her life. Instead, I asked her to embrace it. I offered her help to give up her perfectionism, judgmental attitude, criticism, and negativity. She needed help; I offered it; then it was up to her to decide if she was going to accept it.

This is the critical third step to help. Once the need for help is acknowledged and offered, you still must make a decision to accept the help. When you do, your life becomes linked with the person who offered the help. A relationship of trust is established. Help is offered, but you must reach out, take it, and incorporate it into your life. When you do, you are changed.

I am pleased to say that Denise accepted my offer of help and was changed. She let me in past all of those "No Trespassing" signs, into the deep hurt, disappointments, frustrations, and betrayals in her life. Little by little, she came to embrace her weaknesses instead of running away from them. By accepting herself, with all of her flaws that she'd tried so desperately to hide, she was able to begin to accept other people as no better or worse than herself. Anger and bitterness dispersed, and she was able to relax and learn to love herself and others. Experiencing love, she was able to resist substituting food for it. Experiencing love, she was able to draw closer to God.

EVER-PRESENT HELP

Psalm 46:1 says, "God is our refuge and strength, an ever-present help in trouble." There are so many ways God has promised to provide us with help. I don't know about your life specifically, but I know, in general, I'm always in need of help. I guess that's why I like the phrase "ever-present" in this verse. It means to me that God is always watching, always aware, always there for me.

Hebrews 13:6 sums it up pretty well: "So we say with confidence, 'The Lord is my helper; I will not be afraid. What can man do to me?'"

Planting Seeds

Think about where you are in the three steps of help. Please recognize that you may be at different steps on different issues in your life. In order to help you identify just where you are, I'd like you to write down the areas in your life where you know you need help. As you've worked through this book and other Planting Seeds sections, these will be areas you've identified as sources of fuel for your excessities. Again, they could be anger, loneliness, frustration, lack of self-control, lack of motivation, relationships, food, or addictions. By this time, you should be aware of the issues that send you running to your favorite excessity.

I need help with …

1.

2.

3.

4.

5.

Given your list above (which can be more or less than five), I'd like you to think about what help has been offered. Using the items in the above list as the subjects below, list what sort of help you've turned to and where it's come from. This could be help from all kinds of different sources, whether true help or not.

Help for:

1. _____

What I've used for help:

2. _____

What I've used for help:

3. _____

What I've used for help:

4. _____

What I've used for help:

5. _____

What I've used for help:

Looking over what you've used for help in each of these areas, place a line through any that proved to be false, and put an "F" next to it. These would be the kind of help offered that failed to deliver on its promises, that ended up literally being more trouble than it was worth. For those things that have proved truly helpful to you, circle these and put a "T" by each. They could be things, attitudes, people, or beliefs. This is true help that's been offered and accepted. This help has changed you as a person. Reflect briefly on how each of these helps has changed you:

How I've been changed:

As you think over your issues and the help that's been offered and accepted, are there still some things left on the table? Are you afraid to accept some help because of what you'd have to give up and how you would be changed in the process? Don't be afraid to admit your hesitation, your fear, your resistance to this type of help. Remember, little by little, baby steps. Be honest about what those things are.

I'm not ready to give up my …

1.

2.

3.

4.

5.

Perhaps, in order to help you accept help in these tough areas, it would be a good exercise to go over all the ways God provides help as described in the first ten psalms. I'd like you read over the list and think about how you'd feel with this kind of help in your own life. Think about each one, but circle any that just tug at your heart, any you feel a strong connection to in your own life. This could take you a while. I'd like you to get out a separate piece of paper and write at least a paragraph under each. Answer the questions, and see where those answers lead you. If it's too much to do in one sitting (and it will be for most people, so don't worry), come back to it. If you insist upon *not* writing (yes, I know you're out there!), at least meditate and think about each.

As a *refuge* (2:12): Are there times you need a place to run to for shelter? Are there thoughts and desires you'd like a refuge from? How would a place of refuge be helpful to you?

As a *shield* (3:3): Do you ever feel exposed and vulnerable? Do you ever feel a need to be shielded? From what or whom?

As someone who *answers* (3:4): Are there times when you cry out and no one seems to listen? Are there times people listen but no one bothers to answer? How would answers in your life be helpful?

As someone who *sustains* (3:5): Do you ever feel sometimes like you're barely able to put one foot in front of the other? What could you do in your life if you were being constantly sustained?

As a *deliverer* (3:7–8): Ever find yourself in so much trouble you couldn't see any way out? If a deliverer could come to your rescue right now, what would you leave totally behind?

As a *relief* (4:1): Excessities are all about the promise of relief, with little of the fulfillment. What would be a relief in your life right now?

As a source of *joy* (4:7): When is the last time you felt real joy in your life? How often do you feel joyful? When real joy comes, do you always feel a little guilty or fearful you'll have to somehow pay for the joy in your life? How would an attitude of joy be helpful?

As a source of *peace* (4:8): When is the last time you felt a sense of peace in your life? How long did it last? What interrupted it? What would you give up in order to have a life of peace? What have you exchanged in your life today for peace? How is that bargain going? Are you experiencing true peace?

As a source of *safety* (4:8): Where do you find safety today? Where have you found safety in the past? If you could feel safe from something, what would it be? If you didn't have to worry about being unsafe or vulnerable, what changes would you make in your life?

As a source of *mercy* (5:7): All of us do things we are ashamed of because we mess up and hurt ourselves or others. How much time and energy do you use blaming yourself over things you've done? How much time and energy do you use being ashamed of who you are, where you came from, or what you've done in your life? If you could be assured of mercy, forgiveness, and grace, how would that affect your life and how you feel about yourself?

As a *leader* (5:8): As you think over areas in your life, where do you need to step down as leader, as the one in charge? Where are you afraid to turn over leadership? In what ways have you already turned over areas of your life to the leadership of other people or other things?

As a *protector* (5:11): Who have been your protectors in your life? How did you feel when you were around them? Is there anyone you are a protector for? If you knew you were protected, how would this help you live your life and make decisions?

As a source of *blessing* (5:12): Did you know that God's desire is not to harm you but to bless you? Some people coming from a faith-community background have gotten this backward. They believe that God is a source of condemnation, punishment, and retribution. They believe that God only blesses the perfect and the righteous— in other words, other people but not them. Are you one who thinks this way? How could God bless your life right now? What would it take to trust Him enough to ask? What would it take to believe you would receive it?

As a source of *justice* (7:6): Have you been treated unfairly? When? By whom or what? Do you feel justice was denied you? If you felt justice was done, could you put the pain and anger aside? If you could put the pain and anger aside, how would this help you in your life?

As a source of *security* (7:9): It's amazing what sorts of things people will anchor themselves to in order to feel secure. What do you anchor yourself to when things get stormy? How effective is this anchor? How long term is this anchor? If this anchor were to be uprooted tomorrow, where would you turn for security?

As a source of *majesty* (8:1): Do you ever look for the transcendent in your life, for an experience outside of yourself? If so, where do you turn to get it? Do you ever wish you could lose yourself in something else, even if just for a little while? What do you "get lost" in? How do you feel when you "come back to earth" and it's just you again?

As a *stronghold* (9:9): Do you ever wish for a place where you could face the world or your fears or your enemies from a position of strength? How would it be helpful to have such a place from which to defend yourself, where you knew your back was covered and reinforcements were at the ready?

As a source of *trust* (9:10): What do you trust in your life? Who do you trust in your life? Do you trust yourself? How important is trust to you?

As an *avenger* (9:12): Wrongs just seem that way—*wrong*. There is great satisfaction in being avenged. It is as if the world is set back into proper motion and things returned to the way they should be when wrongs are righted. If you could have something set right, what would it be?

As the *hope* of the afflicted (9:18): Affliction is persistent suffering or anguish. In this chronic state of distress, I'm not sure there's anything more helpful than hope. Are you afflicted by something that's happened to you? Do you have hope in the midst of your suffering? If so, what do you hope for? What do you need to endure the suffering? What would your life be like if this suffering were to end?

As the *helper* of the fatherless (10:14): Too many children grow up in this world without a father or without the presence of their fathers in their lives. This is a tragedy I see played out over and over again with adult children. If you are without your father, for whatever reason, do you know how much God wants to be your father? Do you know how much He loves you as a father? If you could know this, believe it, and feel it, what holes in your heart would this heal?

As the *defender* of the oppressed (10:18): Oppressed people are the very definition of those who need help. Oppression occurs when someone or something stronger than you injures you in some way. You aren't able to defend yourself because of the very nature of the oppression. How have you been oppressed in your life? Did anyone come to your defense? Do you believe that God will come to your defense?

Congratulations on working through this section. I know it wasn't easy or quick, but there's an important point I want to make. God has promised to be your helper, to provide you with all of the following: a *refuge*, a *shield*, *answers*, *sustenance*, *deliverance*, *relief*, *joy*, *peace*, *safety*, *mercy*, *leadership*, *protection*, *blessing*, *justice*, *security*, *majesty*, a *stronghold*, *trust*, *vengeance*, *hope in affliction*, the love of a *father*, and *defense*. And these promises are just a small portion from a very long book. With all of these things in your life, can't you see how they would crowd out the need for anything else? God alone wants to be your helper. He is tired of you running to the idols of your excessities for all of these things. Is He jealous? Yes. He also knows those things are mere blocks of wood, useless to provide the help He can.

You've already come to understand the falsity of so many of the things you turn to for help in your life. Take the necessary steps, and get the true help you need. I'd like you to write down three places you can go for help. For me, when I need help in my life, I know I can go to family, trusted friends, mentors, and my faith community. I also know I can go to God through prayer, His Word, and by connecting to His Spirit. What about you?

Where I can go for true help:

1.

2.

3.

If you feel you're a bit lacking in the true-help category, perhaps it's time to invest some of that time you've spent on the pursuit of your excessities in developing a better, stronger framework of help. Building up healthy relationships with yourself, others, and God is always a worthwhile effort.

> *Father God, help me! Help me know*
> *what I need in my life. Help me see*
> *what it is You want to give me. Help me*

*accept the help You offer. Remind me
when I'm being rebellious and seeking
after an idol of my own making. Allow
Your Holy Spirit to fill my life and my
heart. Allow Your Spirit to whisper Your
words and Your truth into my innermost
parts. Help me recognize Your voice
and the work of Your Spirit in my life.*

14

God Provides Answers

*This is what the LORD says, he who made the
earth, the LORD who formed it and established
it—the LORD is his name. "Call to me and I will
answer you and tell you great and unsearchable
things you do not know." (Jer. 33:2–3)*

There is something profoundly unsettling about an unanswered question. A question is a form of need; a question is a need for an answer. Needs have a way of becoming progressively louder and louder the longer they go unanswered. The longer a question goes unanswered, the harder it is to believe there was ever an answer in the first place. When things appear to have no answer, no reason for happening, the world becomes unhinged. When your world becomes unhinged, when your life appears adrift upon a turbulent and disconnected world, there is no telling what you'll reach out for in order to find something, anything, to hold on to. That's where excessities come in; they are grab-able, easily accessible handholds, as we've seen.

Unanswered questions are a casualty of being in this world. Maybe they're a part of the "trouble" Jesus says we will inevitably have. They're a reality we have to deal with now, but this won't always be so. Paul says in 1 Corinthians 13:12, "Now we see but a poor reflection as in a mirror; then we shall see face to face. Now I know in part; then I shall know fully, even as I am fully known." There is a time for every question to be answered; we're just not there yet. So what do we do in the meantime? If unanswered questions and the turmoil they produce have the power to propel us toward useless excessities, is there a way to stay grounded without having the answer to every question, even the deeper ones?

The way I stay grounded when I don't know the answer, even when I really need to know the answer, is to rest in the faith that God knows even if I don't. This doesn't mean that God is somehow obligated by the Jeremiah passage that started this chapter to tell me everything I ask. This isn't some sort of cosmic math formula with my question and God's knowledge required to equal an answer. I've got to factor in Isaiah 55:8: "'For my thoughts are not your thoughts, neither are your ways my ways,' declares the LORD." Sometimes the answer is, frankly, out of my league. Trusting that there is an answer, even when I don't know it or God chooses not to reveal it, requires another one of those leaps of faith. In my experience, sometimes the courage to make the leap is enough of an answer in itself.

While the Jeremiah passage isn't an equation, it is a promise. It's also very much in line with how God interacts with us. He is all about knowing the truth and revealing that truth. He's all about giving answers. That's pretty much what Jesus did for the three years He was ministering here, walking around on the earth. He spent His time showing people why He was sent, what He was sent to do, where He came from and where He was going, when He would be leaving and when He would return, how to respond to the truth He presented, and who sent Him in the first place. He fulfilled all of the question words—*why, what, where, when, how,* and *who*—with answers.

Perhaps you remember the television show *The X-Files,* which ran from 1993 to 2002. It was a very strange science-fiction type of show about two FBI agents, Mulder and Scully, who went around trying to find out the truth about bizarre phenomena. The tagline of the show was *the truth is out there.* Of course, the truth of the show was complete fiction, but I've always liked the tagline. The truth *is* out there; the truth is God. Sometimes that's all the truth, all the answer, we get to the questions we have—God is. Or, as He put it in the Old Testament, I AM.

OUTSIDE YOUR BOX

Because I deal with the answers to difficult questions, I have always been fascinated by a particular exchange between Jesus and His disciples in the book of John. The disciples had the benefit of walking along with Jesus and receiving answers to their questions, of which, quite naturally, there were many. Mark 4:34 says that Jesus made it a point to explain *everything* to the disciples in private. That's a pretty amazing statement! Of course, while the verse says that Jesus explained everything, it doesn't say the disciples understood everything. There can be a lag time between explanation and understanding—sometimes a matter of moments; other times a matter of years.

During this particular exchange in John 9, Jesus and His disciples are walking along, and the disciples ask Jesus a variation of the classic *why do bad things happen* question. As they were walking, they saw a blind man and asked Jesus why the man had been born blind. They assumed it was because of some sin, either the man's or the man's parents'—a prevalent opinion in those days. As we often do, they were trying to assess blame in a tragic circumstance. Jesus' answer, I'm sure, was surprising. He says in verse 3 that no one's sin was responsible for the man being blind. Instead, Jesus says that the man's blindness occurred so that "the work of God might be displayed in his life" (John 9:3).

The answer to the *why* is that *God allowed it to happen.* This can, on the surface, be a very harsh reality to digest. However, I think it goes even further than that. The operative truth here is not that God allows bad things to happen to people; the operative truth here is that God allows bad things to happen to people *knowing* He has the capacity, the love, the ability to turn that bad thing into something else, something so extraordinary God Himself is displayed within it for all to see. It's always been interesting to me that Jesus would use the circumstance of blindness to illustrate a kind of vision—the powerful way God can be seen in someone's life. The focus according to the disciples was the blindness. The focus according to Jesus was the power of God.

I don't want to carry the vision analogy too far, but being caught up in the swirl of excessities is like living with blinders on. All you can see is the excessity; it's the one thing you focus on. Your excessity becomes your blindness. If God can use a man's blindness to display His power, He can do it for you. How do I know? Because I've seen it. This is what happens when someone consumed by anorexia trusts God and begins to eat again. It's what happens when someone

devoted to drugs trusts God instead. It's what happens when someone
determined to drown out the scream of pain through any number
of numbing activities stops long enough to really listen. These are
miracles, no less than the healing that took place through Jesus.

The answer to your *why* or *what* or *where* or *when* or *how* or *who*
may come in the form of a miracle. Giving up your excessity and
choosing to walk a different path are nothing short of the working
of God displayed in your life, nothing short of the power of God in
your life. Excessities, as we've seen, are powerful. They create their
own centrifugal force. Breaking free of that force requires an even
greater power. It's the power Alcoholics Anonymous calls a "higher
Power." You've been living your life displaying the power of your
excessities. Isn't it time to turn things around and start displaying the
power of God?

POINTING THE WAY

One of the most rewarding things about my work is seeing a person
struggling with some sort of addiction overcome it and then turn the
pit he or she has just climbed out of into a platform to lift others.
Each victory is an affirmation of the next one. I can't always tell who
that next victory will be, but I know that person is coming.

As you think about your life without your time, energy, and
resources being poured down that sinkhole of excessities, I'd like
you to consider how you can encourage others. One of the most
powerful tools we use in recovery at The Center is the victory of
others who have walked down the same road. When those who are
suffering meet, hear, and experience firsthand someone who has been

successful, it gives them hope. It also gives the speaker a purpose, a way to redeem his or her experience.

There is something so powerful about intentionally turning the focus of your life from a narrow field of vision on self and expanding it out to encompass all that God has planned and purposed for you. He never intended for you to live within a shrunken world, within a tight little spiral of spinning excessities. The truth is out there, and it's a greater life for you. Your life has been planned by God from the beginning to display His power. Philippians 2:13 says that God is at work in you according to His good purpose. He's got a purpose for you. But when you stick to your excessities, you hold back what He has planned for you. The truth of your life in God is out there, and the life He has purposed for you is one where excessities have no place.

Planting Seeds

As you've worked through this book, you've come face-to-face with many of the questions and answers that make up the fabric of your life. You've come to know yourself better and understand many of the *whys* behind what you do. What answers have you been shown by God? What truths have been revealed to you? Go back through the earlier Planting Seeds sections, and specifically look for these answers, these truths. Look for truths that specifically contradict the falsehoods that fuel your excessities. Look for answers to help you overcome your anger, addictions, fears, shame, loneliness, sadness, insecurities, need for control, need for comfort, desire for pleasure, or whatever it is you've identified as pushing excessities to the forefront of your life.

My truths:

Living a life devoted to your excessities is not your purpose on this earth, even if they involve work or status or affirmation of some kind. Finding your satisfaction, comfort, pleasure, validation, reassurance, security, or control through a manufactured behavior, attitude, or activity is not what God has in mind for you. He wants to be the source of all those things. What these things can bring you are just cheap imitations compared to the work of God that can be displayed.

Incorporating these truths above, what do you envision for your life? What sorts of things would you like to do? Do you feel called in particular to something? What do you see as your purpose for living on this earth, in this place, right now? What do you dream of doing? What do you aspire to? If this is difficult for you to consider, start small. What is one small thing you would like to be able to do?

What I want for my life:

I would venture to say that staying stuck in your excessities is not helping you to get any closer to what you want for your life. Most of you should honestly be able to admit that your excessities exist like a weight upon your shoulders. They keep you trapped and chained to all of the negative things in your life. Freedom means being able to finally grow into the person and the purpose God has intended for you from the beginning.

When people become unchained from their excessities, they are able to dream again. It can be difficult at first because even thinking about a positive tomorrow is such a foreign concept. If that's the case for you, I'd like you to consider your next book after this one. I'd like you to consider going through Rick Warren's *The Purpose-Driven Life: What on Earth Am I Here For?* If you haven't read it, I urge you to. I found it extremely helpful, insightful, and inspirational. If you're looking for even more answers for your life, this book may help point you to them.

If you've already read it, I urge you to pick it up and read it again. This time, I'd like you to read it from a vision of your life without the constraints of your excessities. If you do not intentionally seek out new ways to fill up your life, the pull of your excessities will have a greater chance to drag you back down.

Excessities are powerful, but so are dreams and aspirations. These have motivated people to do extraordinary things. It's time to begin to crowd your life with positive, uplifting, purposeful plans of God. You want a crowd of positives so packed in around you that all your former excessities will be able to do is catch a glimpse of your life from the periphery. You want them so far from the core of your being, all they can do is jump up and down at the edges, without any way to weasel themselves back inside.

> God of truth, God of answers, I turn to
> You now. I praise You for the answers
> You've already revealed to me. I ask

You to continue to speak Your truth into my life. Help me know what questions I need to ask. Help me hear Your voice when You answer. If I don't understand, be patient with me. If I don't understand, help me be patient with You. When I have to wait for Your answer, increase my faith and trust in You. I thank You that You never give me an answer impossible to handle, even when it feels that way. When it feels that way, remind me how very much You love me.

Afterword

The end of a matter is better than its beginning,
and patience is better than pride. (Eccl. 7:8)

Well, you've made it through. Hopefully, you've done the work, opened up your heart and mind, and begun to take those baby steps toward freedom from your excessities. My part in this is small; I can only point you in the right direction. You're the one who has to take the steps. Remember, though, that you don't have to try to take them all at once. Start small and keep going. It's a journey that will require patience, as the verse above says. Fueled by patience and not pride, keep going.

Don't get discouraged if you take a step backward. Figure out what prompted you to return to the vomit, as Proverbs 26:11 says, and *learn* from it. Gain understanding and insight. Use what you learn from that backward step as a way to propel you even further forward. With each step you take, including a backward step now and then, you'll be traveling closer to the end of the matter, putting an end to the power and control these excessities have over your life.

Learn from your mistakes, and become stronger, become wiser about yourself. In doing so, you'll be exchanging the current relationship you have with your excessities for an even deeper and more intimate relationship with yourself and with God. I've been thinking a lot about relationships lately because of what my cousin John is going through. John has inoperable cancer, and his life is ebbing away daily. Believe me, his time and his energy are not devoted to chasing after excessities. His mind is not consumed with how he is going to engage in this or that *thing* to make him feel better. Instead, he is using his energies to stay close to God and prepare himself and his family for his death.

Listen to something John recently wrote: "None of us knows when we will die. It is true that I know my date is drawing close, but none of us knows if your date may be closer than mine. The key here is to be ready all the time." Can you admit that you've lived your life merely ready to engage in your excessities and not really ready for much more important things?

Wasting your time on excessities does nothing to help you be ready for life, or death. At the end of his life, John gets that. The line between his needs and wants has become very clear. My prayer for you is you won't wait that long. John is getting ready to die; my admonition to you as you finish this book is to *get ready to live!*

Eugene Peterson puts it this way in *The Message:*

> Don't waste your time on useless work,
> mere busywork, the barren pursuits of
> darkness. Expose these things for the
> sham they are. It's a scandal when people
> waste their lives on things they must do
> in the darkness where no one will see. Rip

the cover off those frauds and see how attractive they look in the light of Christ. Wake up from your sleep, climb out of your coffins; Christ will show you the light! So watch your step. Use your head. Make the most of every chance you get. (Eph. 5:11–16)

Believe me, after a quarter century in this business, I know how hard it is to change behavior. Every time you are confronted with a choice between what you *want* to do and what you know you *need* to do, make the most of that chance. Choose wisely and move forward. If you take a step backward, learn from it and grow; use your head. Above all, keep going, keep progressing in your understanding of yourself and what you truly need. Keep progressing in your understanding of where to go to truly meet that need. I think, in the end, you'll discover what my cousin John has—in the end, it really comes down to you and God, which is a very good thing when it comes to needs. In Matthew 6:8, Jesus reassures you that God's got you covered in that department; He already knows what you need even before you ask.

I cannot thank you enough for taking this small journey with me. I applaud your willingness to be vulnerable and your openness to change; that's rare in this world. I've ended each chapter in this book with a prayer. Here is my prayer for you—

May God astonish you with His sufficiency for all your needs.

May He humble you with His generosity
for the desires of your heart.

Dr. Gregg Jantz

Notes

CHAPTER 2:

1. Stephen Stills, "Love the One You're With," Stephen Stills © 1970 Atlantic Records.

2. Nora Volkow, "From the Director," National Institute on Drug Abuse: Research Report Series, July 2001, www.drugabuse.gov/PDF/RRPrescription.pdf.

3. "Prescription Medications," National Institute on Drug Abuse, www.nida.nih.gov/DrugPages/prescription.html.

4. Ibid.

5. Dr. Gregg Jantz, *Turning the Tables on Gambling* (Colorado Springs, CO: Shaw Books, 2001).

6. "Twenty Questions: How Do I Know If I'm a Workaholic?" Workaholics Anonymous, www.workaholics-anonymous.org/page.php?page=knowing.

7. "Twenty Questions," Gamblers Anonymous, www.gamblersanonymous.org/20questions.html.

8. "Self Assessment," Sex Addicts Anonymous, http://saa-recovery.org/IsSAAForYou/SelfAssessment.

CHAPTER 3:

1. Robert Frost, "Nothing Gold Can Stay," *The Poetry of Robert Frost*, ed. Edward Connery Lathem (New York: Henry Holt and Company, 1969).

CHAPTER 4:

1. "The Numbers Count: Mental Disorders in America," National Institute of Mental Health, www.nimh.nih.gov/health/publications/ the-numbers-count-mental-disorders-in-america/index.shtml.

2. "Generalized Anxiety Disorder," National Institute of Mental Health, www.nimh.nih.gov/health/topics/generalized-anxiety-disorder-gad/index.shtml.

3. "Panic Disorder," National Institute of Mental Health, www.nimh.nih.gov/health/topics/panic-disorder/index.shtml.

4. "Obsessive-Compulsive Disorder, OCD," National Institute of Mental Health, www.nimh.nih.gov/health/topics/obsessive-compulsive-disorder-ocd/index.shtml.

5. "Post-Traumatic Stress Disorder (PTSD)," National Institute of Mental Health, www.nimh.nih.gov/health/topics/post-traumatic-stress-disorder-ptsd/index.shtml.

6. "The Numbers Count: Mental Disorders in America," National Institute of Mental Health, www.nimh.nih.gov/health/publications/ the-numbers-count-mental-disorders-in-america/index.shtml.

7. "Social Phobia (Social Anxiety Disorder)," National Institute of Mental Health, www.nimh.nih.gov/health/topics/social-phobia-social-anxiety-disorder/index.shtml.

CHAPTER 7:

1. "The Twelve Steps of Alcoholics Anonymous," A.A. World Services, Inc., www.aa.org/en_pdfs/smf-121_en.pdf.

CHAPTER 12:

1. William Shakespeare, *Hamlet,* ed. Richard Grant White et al. (New York: Houghton, Mifflin and Company, 1897), 1.5.167. References are to act, scene, and line.

Books by Gregory L. Jantz, PhD

Gotta Have It! Freedom from Wanting Everything Right Here, Right Now (David C. Cook, 2010)

Hope, Help, and Healing for Eating Disorders (Waterbrook/Shaw, revised 2002, revised 2010)

Every Woman's Guide to Anger (Revell, 2009)

Healing the Scars of Emotional Abuse (Revell, revised 2009)

Happy for the Rest of Your Life (Strang, 2009)

How to De-Stress Your Life (Spire, 2008)

The Body God Designed (Strang, 2008)

The Molding of a Champion (New Leaf Press, 2007)

Healthy Habits, Happy Kids (Revell, 2005)

Total Temple Makeover (Howard, 2005)

Thin Over 40 (Penguin, 2004)

Losing Weight Permanently (Spire, 2004, 2010)

Moving Beyond Depression: A Whole Person Approach to Healing (Waterbrook/Shaw, 2003)